IMPROVE YOUR POKER

by
BOB CIAFFONE

A WELL-KNOWN PROFESSIONAL PLAYER AND WRITER EXPLAINS HOW TO PLAY TOP-CLASS POKER

♠ ♥ ♦ ♣ ♠ ♥ ♦ ♣ ♠ ♥ ♦ ♣ ♠ ♥ ♦ ♣ ♠ ♥ ♦ ♣ ♠ ♥ ♦ ♣ ♠ ♥ ♦ ♣ ♠ ♥ ♦ ♣

♠ ♥ ♦ ♣ ♠ ♥ ♦ ♣ ♠ ♥ ♦ ♣ ♠ ♥ ♦ ♣ ♠ ♥ ♦ ♣ ♠ ♥ ♦ ♣ ♠ ♥ ♦ ♣ ♠ ♥ ♦ ♣

DEDICATION

I would like to dedicate this book to my parents, Alfred and Marjorie Ciaffone. My mother, who died in 1995, was the person who first taught me the game. She did this in September of 1950, when I was not yet ten years old. Both of my parents have always been supportive of me regardless of the direction I have chosen to take my life. For this kind help I am expressing my gratitude here.

♠ ♥ ♦ ♣ ♠ ♥ ♦ ♣ ♠ ♥ ♦ ♣ ♠ ♥ ♦ ♣ ♠ ♥ ♦ ♣ ♠ ♥ ♦ ♣ ♠ ♥ ♦ ♣ ♠ ♥ ♦ ♣

TABLE OF CONTENTS

TABLE OF CONTENTS (cont.)

TABLE OF CONTENTS (cont.)

ABOUT THIS BOOK

As of the time this book is first published, in 1997, I have been playing poker for 47 years. Part of my income has been derived from poker ever since I was a teenager, and through the years that proportion continued to increase, so it is hard to pinpoint the exact moment you could call me a professional player. But for the last two decades, poker has been my primary source of income. Most of my poker career has been spent playing in major poker cities like Dallas, Las Vegas, and Los Angeles. I have also on occasion traveled a long way to find a good poker game. Some of my most interesting experiences have come at poker tables in such diverse places as Halifax, London, Malta, and Katmandu. So for sure you are getting advice from a seasoned veteran.

"Improve Your Poker" is a blend of material from several sources. A lot of it is taken from articles I've written over the years for publications such as "Card Player," "Sports Form," "Poker Player," and "Gambling Times." Some of it is information that so far I have preferred to reveal only in subscription newsletters. Naturally, since I give private poker lessons, a portion of what I have prepared for my students is included. Finally, there is some new writing prepared specially for this book. All of the material has been carefully edited and organized for your convenience. I would urge you to read even the chapters about poker forms you do not play, as some ideas presented in those chapters will also be applicable to the forms of poker you prefer. Even though my book is a series of articles on important poker concepts for serious players rather than a all-encompassing work covering every aspect of the game, I am sure you will like it.

I know why you are reading this book. You want to put some extra money into your pocket. My book will help you. I have had a long writing career, and have discussed a wide range of poker topics. My previous writing has covered such diverse subjects as cardroom management, the running of poker tournaments, various traveling adventures, and prominent poker personalities. I am a

ABOUT THIS BOOK

leading authority on poker rules, have authored several rulebooks, and written many articles on that subject. My proudest achievement in writing about gambling is a paper called "A Comparative Study Of State Laws On Social Gambling," which examines gambling laws in all the states, and demonstrates that about half the states have some laws that are seriously flawed. But there is no material on such subjects in this book. Everything in here is directed to answering one question; "How can I improve my poker game?"

Have you ever wondered why there are so many bad poker players? My friend poker pro O'Neil Longson, seeing a weak player just giving his money away, sometimes says quietly, "Where do they come from?" Part of the reason there are so many bad players is because good information about how to play professional level poker is hard to obtain. Where can you get what you need?

If you want high-quality information, you should go to someone who has it. You don't go to a street corner bum to get stock market advice. There are plenty of hackers dispensing what passes for "poker wisdom." If you want to become a fellow hacker, they'll tell you how. If you want to become a top poker player, better get your assistance from somebody who already is where you are trying to go.

This book contains a large amount of top-quality poker advice. In it techniques and concepts are discussed that are used by the best professional poker players. I think you will enjoy reading "Improve Your Poker," and be able to use it to take a long stride toward attaining your poker goal. I feel confident anyone will be a better player after studying it, no matter how well he or she may already play.

FOLLOW YOUR ABC'S

Don't think the low-limit novice has a monopoly on bad play. There is plenty of it in the higher-limit games, even some by professional players. Time after time, I see people who should know better—even people who **do** know better—making fundamental errors. Note that these types of errors are the ones that are the most detrimental to your bankroll. Here are what may be the three most common and damaging mistakes in poker.

(A) Playing too many starting hands. This mistake is common to beginner and expert alike. It is also the most detrimental of all the poker mistakes. The most basic element of poker is betting that your hand is better than the other guy's. The stronger starting hand wins more pots. If you play thirty percent of the hands dealt, and the opponents play half that many, you are going uphill. Sure, it is possible to gun your way out of trouble some of the time by betting until the opposition caves in. This does not mean that you should court trouble. In any form of poker, there are plenty of ways to get into trouble and have to gun your way out even when playing first-rate hands. Ask any pot-limit hold'em player who ever raised on A-K suited and missed the flop. Why voluntarily get into trouble by playing second-rate hands? If you are losing at poker, it is almost surely because you are not properly applying the most important weapon in your poker arsenal—the fold.

(B). Going on tilt. This expression refers to going out of control because you are losing. Many players are good front-runners. It is easier to play well when you are running a little lucky. The real test of discipline is how you play when losing, especially if longshot hands are cashing against you. It is tempting to say, "I'll give them a dose of their own medicine," and play a trashy hand. The likely result is to dig yourself a hole too big to get out of. The way to avoid steaming is to say to yourself, "The cards are going to turn eventually; maybe real soon. If I don't get stuck too much, I can probably get out of this trap."

(C) Failing to back good hands strongly enough. Some people play poker like Timid Tim. I saw a guy in my pot-limit Omaha game being raised and reraised on the flop by two players who had turned a straight. He held top set and the nut flush-draw, and failed to go all-in because he "needed to draw out." By holding back, he let the opponents get away from their hands when he filled up or made a flush.

This example was an unusual situation. I'm sure hardly any of you are that cautious with such a monster hand. However, I often see people fail to raise at Omaha with excellent hands such as Q♠-J♠-10♦-8♣ or A♠-K♥-J♠-8♥. Hands like these don't grow on trees. It is a weak policy to wait for a good flop before committing any sizable money on quality hands. If you are going to out-wait the opposition and start with better hands, it is obviously good sense to be willing to back those hands with a raise.

My three tips were certainly not profound, were they? Play good hands, don't go on tilt when losing, and back your good hands with strong betting. This kind of advice can be found in any beginning poker book. There is a lot more to poker than these simple platitudes, but **these other things are not nearly as important**.

Many experienced players know the whole poker alphabet all the way to Z, yet they still have trouble with A, B, and C. Anybody can be a winning player by playing only in good games, and following their ABC's. The frills add to your win, but the biggest determinant of whether you win or lose is whether you are following these three basic principles of proper play.

FOUR POKER MYTHS

There are a number of myths that have grown up about the necessary ingredients for success at poker. A myth usually has a germ of truth to it, with a large degree of distortion. It sounds plausible, but a close examination will reveal that there is more falsehood than truth. The overall effect of these poker myths is to mislead people who are trying to improve their game. Here are my candidates for the four misleading myths that do the most damage to players' bankrolls—especially newbies:

(1) You've got to advertise.
This gets misinterpreted into meaning that you need to bluff a lot so your good hands will make mucho money. My quarrel with this thinking is that the purpose of a bluff is to win the pot. It may not work, but there should be a reasonable chance of success. Those who bluff to advertise bluff too often and in situations where success is remote. A little bit of bluffing is enough to get you action on your good hands. Advertising is only a byproduct of bluffing, not the main purpose.

(2) Confidence is very important for a player.
Even though it is helpful in any endeavor to have confidence, we must ask, "Where does that confidence come from?" When you see Tiger Woods get up on that eighteenth tee on national television and whack a big drive right down the middle, he looks confident. The reason for this confidence is certainly not that he hits slices into the boondocks on the practice tee, but thinks he can do well under pressure. No, no, no. The reason is he has performed so well on previous occasions that he feels he can do the same thing when the chips are down.

I would argue that it is vital for a poker player—or any gambler—to have a realistic view of his own strength. Should a $5-$10 limit player go into a trance, mumble fifty times to himself "I am the greatest," and then take a seat in a tough $50-$100 game?

FOUR POKER MYTHS

Would you want to stake him? Confidence is something that flows naturally as a result of successes. You don't swell your chest with confidence and then become successful; it's the other way around. The maxim should read, "A realistic appraisal of one's abilities is important for a player."

(3) The best players are all super-aggressive.
This is simply not true. There are only a few successful players that are super-aggressive. These players are better performers at tournament play than money play, and also are better at big-bet poker than limit play. Three-time World Champion Stu Ungar is a good example of this.

A look at the guys who get the money year after year shows that being selectively aggressive works better than unrelenting pressure, if steady long-term results are the criterion. Look at such players as Chip Reese and Daniel Harrington to see what I mean.

Moreover, even when this hyper-aggressive style is made to work, it will surely not be harnessed by ordinary mortals like you or me. You need to be a real poker genius to know how to extricate yourself from the tough situations this style of play will continually place you. I'll guarantee you the ten most aggressive poker players in America are all busted! Don't be a wimp, but don't try to play in fast forward the whole session either.

(4) You must pay to learn.
This saying makes it sound like you need to blow thousands of dollars to become a good enough player just to break even. While this maxim certainly applies if you feel the need to start playing right away for high stakes, I don't believe it applies to low stakes—which is the level where most beginners belong. The cheap poker games have a lot of undisciplined players. I believe newcomers can at least break even simply by reading a book on poker and playing only good hands. The shield of good starting hands should be enough for somebody to hold his own at games below $5-$10 limit, even without knowing the fine points of poker.

FOUR POKER MYTHS

What do all four of these poker myths have in common? They encourage players to put more money into the pot than they should. A player who followed all of these axioms would be confidently raising every pot in a high-stakes game. Such a recipe would bring nothing to him except disaster. So the next time you hear, "You've got to pay to learn," ask yourself whose pockets the speaker wants to line with money. My guess he wants to fill his own with your money, not the other way around.

GETTING AN OVERLAY

Where is your overlay? To have an advantage, you must be doing something different than your opponents. To consider yourself a good player, you should have a reasonable idea what good things you are doing to deserve that epithet.

My favorite games are pot-limit Omaha and no-limit hold'em. I believe my good results in those arenas is due in large measure to having the right overall concepts about the game of poker. My strong point is technique, and my weakest point is knowing how an opponent will play certain hands (especially an opponent who has a view of poker that is a little bit cockeyed). Frankly, I think it is easier for most people to learn from players like me than from someone who plays even better than I do. A lot of the top players have some flaws in technique, but are overpoweringly strong in reading opponents. Technique is easier to teach than tremendous table feel.

I feel that the general philosophy I use on each betting round is where I get most of my overlay. Let's talk about each phase of a deal, and what general thoughts should guide you.

A big part of your edge should be starting with better hands than the opposition. In my opinion, even many of the good players involve themselves on more than the optimum number of starting hands. They seem to think that since they play the game better than their opponents, they can afford to start with the same low-quality hands and still show a profit. To me, my selection of superior starting hands is such an important part of my edge I would not want to give that up. The essence of poker is betting that your hand is better than the other guy's. If you play as many hands as he does, how big can your overlay be?

The worst way to play too many hands is calling raises on inadequate values. You need a better hand to call an opponent's raise than you need to raise the pot yourself. To get specific, avoid playing hold'em hands like A-J offsuit or K-10 suited in raised pots. Throw away medium and small pairs most of the time here also, because you are not getting the right price for flopping a set if the pot has been raised, and the extra money in a raised pot holds the other players to stay in, so the best hand at the end gets the money. Two sevens is not likely to be the best hand when the smoke clears, and also has little chance of improvement if you do not flop a set.

After the flop, Most players are insufficiently aggressive when they are in a heads-up or three-handed pot. It is hard to flop a solid hand like top pair or better. Someone has to get the money when nobody has a decent hand. In weak games, the best hand wins when this happens, because the deal gets checked out. In strong games, the player that is willing to bet gets the cheese.

Fourth street play is very important at both hold'em and Omaha. This is where scare-cards freeze up the conservative players. All strong players have good "follow-through." They are willing to back up the money expended on the flop with another barrel. For example, at pot-limit a bet of the pot on fourth street is likely to make an opponent release all but the best drawing hands. A made hand consisting of only one pair also trembles when a second barrel is fired at it. When I am playing no-limit hold'em, I think my biggest overlay is a willingness to fire another barrel on fourth street most of the time.

If fourth street is critical at no-limit hold'em, then fifth street is the key at pot-limit Omaha. When you do not have what appears to be a winning hand, there are numerous opportunities to win the pot with a bet after all the cards are out. The board often allows for the possibility of a hand being out that is better than the opponent 's. Why not represent that hand? At hold'em, a player can deduce that you do not have the nuts by your previous betting. He rarely can do that at Omaha, because of the wide possibilities present in a four-card hand.

To improve your play at poker, it is necessary to examine your habits on each betting round. Employing the proper philosophy of play at the various points in the betting will make a big difference in your results. Having the right general approach to poker is essential. At every form of the game, I believe that approach to be the playing of very few starting hands, but betting aggressively throughout the rest of the deal.

COUNTER-MEASURES

There is often a correlation in strategy between different games. As a chessplayer, I can see where certain principles of good play apply to both chess and poker. An excellent example of this is "Unsound play by the opponent forces **you** to play unsoundly."

Alexander Alekhine, who was the World Champion at chess back when I was born, once played a tournament game where he made a large number of consecutive knight moves in the opening, a clear violation of basic chess principles. When asked why he played that way, he had this to say: "Were I to play in this fashion against sound play by my opponent, I would be duly punished. But my adversary was the first to depart from principle. And in order to punish this transgression to the fullest extent, I was forced to play unconventionally myself."

I feel these words could just as easily been spoken about the game of poker—perhaps even more so. In poker, if you play straight-forwardly against people who are doing something abnormal, they often can use their unsound play to good advantage. Many years ago, I had a friend who did not realize this. He frequently lost against weaker players. After doing so, he would say, "When you play with idiots, you get idiotic results." His mediocre results were due to a failure to adjust his play to the opposition he was facing. The way you play a game should not be "one size fits all."

Here is a situation in poker that illustrates my point. A poker publication gave a hold'em hand to a group of panelists and asked them how they would play it. The hand was a jack-ten offsuit. Their situation was they were in the first seat to the right of the button in a ninehanded $15-30 limit game, and everyone in front of them had folded. What to do?

Every panelist but one preferred to raise the pot with this hand. Some of them indicated that they thought this play virtually automatic. (Calling was considered so inferior it wasn't an option.) My own preference is to throw this dog in the muck more often than not. I don't raise unless there is reason to think the big blind will be reluctant to contest the pot. This hand is clearly not worth a raise on merit alone, as it is unlikely to be the best hand. But my opinion of this hand is not relevant to our discussion. The point is there are many hold'em players who share the opinion of those panelists. In other words, a lot of your opponents are going to try stealing your blind money. Don't let them. Defend yourself against these avaricious animals by playing differently than you would against a sound poker player.

Here are four ways to defeat those thieves when you are in the big blind:

First, you can call their raises with a weaker hand than is your normal practice. Hands such as A♦-4♣, K♠-7♠, 9♥-8♦, and so forth are bad hands that normally should be thrown away facing a solid raise. But against a known thief, you should depart from sound play and call.

Second, if you have a decent hand such as A♠-Q♥ or 7♠-7♣, good enough to raise a limper, play back at the raiser by making it three bets. This is a strong play, because chances are good that you have the best hand, and seizing the initiative places you aggressively for the post-flop betting round. Fight fire with fire.

Third, don't automatically go into a shell if you fail to connect with the flop. People who habitually raise on or near the button on hands like J♠-10♣ don't hit so many flops themselves. You can steal—the more accurate term is resteal—from them by leading out with a bet on the flop, check-raising on the flop, or calling on the flop followed by making a play for the pot on fourth street. Their play is based upon winning all the pots where you don't get immediate help on the board, but there is no reason winning the pots where both players miss the flop should be exclusively the raiser's prerogative, because in this case he is often starting with the weaker hand.

Fourth, when you pick up a big pair, especially aces, you can put on a broken-wing act all the way to the last card. Yes, sometimes they take that dog and beat your two aces. But more often, they keep betting a hand with few or no outs, hoping desperately to get you to fold. After seeing you slowplay a big pair like that, the bullies will think twice about betting automatically every time you check.

Another area where your opponents often depart from optimum play is by trying to save a few bucks via tight folds. If someone thinks you are the rock of Gibraltar simply because you don't play junky starting hands, they can be very vulnerable to a bluff, especially after all the cards are out and they know you're not betting on the come. A bluff at this point is usually getting terrific pot odds. According to game theory, your opponent should call most of the time at limit poker, but some don't. Tight to start doesn't necessarily mean unlikely to bluff. Notice the players who are penny wise and pound foolish; then punish them.

Actually, I believe the principle that unsound play by your opponent is best punished by a departure from normal methods by you actually applies to all games. At backgammon, if your steaming opponent is taking every double, it is usually right to take an extra roll or two before turning the cube, even though you may already have a sound double. At bridge, if your opponents are wild psychers, it pays to adjust your bidding methods to convert some of those cooperative doubles into penalty doubles. At cutthroat pinochle, if one of your opponents is a bidding hog, it sometimes is a good idea to push him up with a bid even though you have no intention of playing the hand, to improve the chance of defeating his final call.

Failing to adjust your normal methods facing unusual behavior leads to less than optimum results. An excellent example is the failure of baseball great Ted Williams to combat the "Boudreau Shift" by hitting to the opposite field. Most baseball authorities agree this stubborn "business as usual" attitude of Williams lowered his batting average by a measurable degree.

In applying the methods we have just discussed, be sure to follow Alekhine's admonitions. These plays are designed to counter unsound actions of your opponents. They were the first to break the principles of sound play. If you try to habitually use these techniques against solid players, you will be going uphill.

12

BEATING A LOOSE GAME

I think there are a lot of players that take a seat in a loose game, get a bad result, and then wonder how such a collection of weak players could ever get their money. To be sure, there is a greater luck factor concerning swings in a loose game, in that the fluctuations are likely to be bigger. The idea is when you beat the game, a good bit of the time, the result will be a huge win. But maybe another factor is also at work. Perhaps you are not playing in an optimum way to take advantage of what appears to be a very favorable gambling situation.

A typical reaction to playing in such a game is this thought process: "These fools are playing such garbage, I can and should play more hands, because I'll still have an overlay. How can you stay out of the pot on a reasonable hand, when you are getting such a good price to play?" This kind of thinking may be getting you into big trouble, depending on the character of the game.

There are actually two types of loose games; we will call them "Type A" and "Type B." In a Type A game, few pots are being raised. As a result, a lot of people are entering the pots on marginal hands. There is a lot of five-way, six-way, and even seven-way action. In such a game, you can lessen your values a little bit, and still be playing better hands than most of your opponents. Note that the two ingredients needed for playing drawing-type hands are both present. You can get in cheaply, and will be facing a large field, insuring a nice payoff if your ship comes in.

It is the Type B game where the problems arise. In this game, there are also a lot of players in the pot on their starting hands (good for drawing hands), but most of the pots are getting raised, and even reraised (very bad for drawing hands). A lot of players use the same style of play for both situations, when in fact our two scenarios are vastly different. In a Type B game, you must have great restraint in entering pots, because the entry fee is two or three times greater than normal. Naturally, most players have the

BEATING A LOOSE GAME

good sense not to be making cold calls in raised and reraised pots. But it is easy to get trapped into paying an exorbitant entry fee if the payments are put on the installment plan. This is another area where poker resembles real life!

Perhaps this is an appropriate moment to discuss how we are using the term "drawing hand," and why it is so important to be paying a cheap entry fee when holding one. Lets use a limit hold'em game as an example. Having the best hand before the flop is not necessarily mean you can win without improvement, or have a better chance than the other players to win the pot. A small pair must buy help to get the cheese. A pair of sixes is a higher-ranking hand than an A-Q, but in a multihanded pot the A-Q is much superior. A "drawing hand" is the way I describe any hand that must improve to win.

Let's discuss that pair of sixes a bit more. It is clearly a drawing hand, because even if nobody has a higher pair in the pocket, it will seldom win without improvement in multihanded raised pots. The extra money holds many of the other players in until the end of the deal; the chances are slim that nobody will be able to beat 6-6 at the finish. Even if a miracle happens and the sixes are good, you don't figure to be still in the pot to claim your winner. How can you call a bet at any point after the flop, when there are only two cards in the deck that will help your hand? To win a multihanded raised pot, you need a two-event parlay. First you must flop a set of sixes, and then you must have them hold up.

The odds on flopping a set are over seven to one against you. That set will get cracked about a quarter of the time. One thing you can depend on; if you flop a set and lose, it will cost you plenty.

I like to see the flop on pocket sixes, but cannot afford to pay through the nose to do it. The long-run odds say that in an unraised pot I need to win about a dozen half-bets just to break even. (We use the term "half-bet" because in a normal betting structure the bet will be twice as much –a full bet –later on in the deal.) If I were guaranteed that it would only cost me one half-bet to play, I would take a chance. But if the pot is raised, it costs me two half-bets, and I now need to win a couple of dozen half-bets just to break even for the times I miss the flop or get a set cracked. This is much harder to do. If I had to call a raise cold, I have a clear fold. But if most of the pots are being raised or reraised, it is foolish to tell yourself, "Maybe I can sneak in for a single bet."

The thinking on any drawing hand should be much the same as your thinking on our example hand of 6-6. To have an overlay, you must see the flop cheaply. This entails not calling a double bet before the flop. In a game where most pots are being raised, it means not falling for the "installment payment" trap. Fold for even a single bet if the pot will likely be raised behind you.

Note that what kinds of hands are raising the pot scarcely enters into your figuring. If you have a drawing hand, the fact that the raiser might have a trashy looking hand like ace-ten offsuit does not help you. Even if the raiser is a maniac with total junk, the fact remains that you need to help in order to win. It actually might be better for you if the raiser had a big pair, as then you figure to get paid off handsomely if you buy help on the flop.

As you can see, in a game where a lot of pots are being raised, you must resist your impulse to go with the flow. When the entry fee is a lot higher, you need a much better hand to play. A loose **wild** game calls for you to tighten up your starting requirements considerably. Otherwise, the overhead you pay to see the flop will be too much to overcome. The fact that there are a lot of other players in is helpful, but not helpful enough to overcome the high cost of seeing the flop. A smart poker player knows there is a huge difference between a loose passive game and a loose wild game. Tighten up to beat the wild ones.

TIGHT AND LOOSE PLAY

In my opinion, the player terms "tight" and "loose" are too vague to convey the information needed for you and I to make an intelligent decision on how to play a hand against a certain opponent. In poker, as in life, typecasting will cause you to err by making an inaccurate generalization about how someone will behave.

As used to describe poker behavior, the term "loose" means often putting money into the pot, and the term "tight" means seldom putting money into the pot. Let's talk about how simply applying such vague terms to your opponent can throw you off on how to play against him.

A concept that I as a no-limit player use quite often but have never seen discussed in print is what I call a player's "call-fold ratio." This concept can also be applied to limit poker.

A player's "call-fold ratio" is the percentage of the time a player will call when he gets popped with a raise representing a strong hand. In other words, I want to know what portion of the time I'm going to get called if I stick some money in a player's face.

Note how poorly the words "tight" or "loose" convey the information I would like to know. Would you rather run a bluff against a tight player or a loose player? Yes, a tight player may be less likely to look you up on suspicion. On the other hand, he is much more likely to be in there on a good hand in the first place, one that can look you up legitimately.

Loose players can actually be subdivided into several categories. For example, I know quite a few hold'em players that like to see a lot of flops. Some of these will bail out rather quickly if they fail to connect. Others simply play loose throughout a hand. These calling stations are hard to bluff.

But I know some tight players that are also hard to bluff. They seem to think, "I waited a long time for this hand, and I'm not going to let some so-and-so run me off it. He's going to have to beat me by showing down a better hand." Certain tight players are also calling stations.

When deciding whether to run a bluff (or bet a drawing hand very strongly), knowing a player's call-fold ratio is quite helpful. Simply watch how each player reacts when he meets strong betting, and get a feel for how often he calls raises. This will help you much more than simply cataloging an opponent as "tight" or "loose."

Another area where the terms 'loose" and "tight" are misapplied is in the area of bluffing. I'm a good example of this. I do not play a lot of starting hands in any form of poker, not even Omaha. Someone watching how often I enter a pot would surely label me a tight player.

But it would be a mistake to continue to apply the appellation tight by jumping to the conclusion that I am simply reluctant to put chips into the pot, and am therefore unlikely to bluff. The fact of the matter is players like me who play few starting hands often try to exploit their tight image to do some thievery. At least, this is true of the better players.

A common poker tactic is to play in a certain manner early in a session, and then change gears later on. This usually means going from loose to tight, as most players use the ploy. The hope is an opponent will pin a label on you, and then fail to adjust when your ship gets tightened.

Failing to notice a player has changed gears is a common poker error. Another time this may happen is when a player starts out as if he had just taken an oath on a bible to play only solid poker, and then suffers some bad beats. This of course will cause most people to loosen up considerably, and an alert opponent should notice when a player is getting metamorphosed this way.

A good player exploits the fact that the poker terms "tight" and "loose" are really overly generalized stereotyping. He does this by noticing if an opponent has pinned such a label on him, and by not pinning such a label on the opponent.

BETTING YOUR HAND

Quite a few poker players have an overly simplistic betting style. When they have a decent hand, they bet. When they have a colossus, they check, planning on check-raising. Poker is not supposed to be played in a knee-jerk reaction fashion. Rather, when holding a fine hand, you should think about what your opponent is likely to have, and what line of play figures to extract the most money from him. Sometimes it is right to check-raise (or even check-call), but often betting right out is your best option.

Let's look at a typical hold'em situation. The game is $10-$20 limit. You are in the big blind holding a pair of eights. The player under the gun opens with a raise, the other players fold, and you of course call. The flop makes you want to burst into a cheery song: 8♠-6♠-2♥. You now hold the top set of three eights, a lock at this point. Should you bet or check?

From an up-front raiser we may expect either an overpair or two big cards such as A-K or A-Q. Let's first see what is likely to happen with each betting method if you are up against an overpair.

If you check, the opponent will bet. Now if you raise, he will call, and continue to call on fourth and fifth street. You may expect to win a total of $60 from him after the flop. A more sophisticated play—and the one most often used—is to check and call on the flop, and check-raise on fourth street. This brings your after-the-flop win from him up to $70, because you got your check-raise in after the limit doubled, thereby winning an extra half a bet.

Suppose you lead right out with your nut hand. Do you really think it is going to go bet-call on every street, and hold your profits down to only $50? No, the betting doesn't go that way any more even in the sociable afternoon home poker game. The overpair is going to raise you at some point. The only question is whether your opponent is going to raise you on the flop or on fourth street.

Here is the way I like to play the hand. If I lead and get raised on the flop, I reraise. He is of course going to call. On fourth

CIRCUS CIRCUS®

HOTEL / CASINO / RENO

FOR ROOM RESERVATIONS CALL TOLL FREE (800) 648-5010

CIRCUS CIRCUS HOTEL/CASINO • LAS VEGAS, NEVADA (800) 634-3450

EXCALIBUR HOTEL/CASINO • LAS VEGAS, NEVADA (800) 937-7777

EDGEWATER HOTEL/CASINO • LAUGHLIN, NEVADA (800) 67-RIVER

COLORADO BELL HOTEL/CASINO • LAUGHLIN, NEVADA (800) 458-9500

street, if something other than a third spade comes, I'm going to check. This will look to him as if I hold a good drawing hand. He is likely to bet, despite my strong wagering on the flop. He will hate to give a free card to a player who is on a draw and has to make a hand on the next card or lose. Even a mouse would probably bet an overpair here. When I check-raise, he is unhappy, and knows the road is uphill. However, he is so far into the hand that he pays it off to the end. This means I am going to win $90, which is obviously better than the check-raise or slowplay methods.

Sometimes the opponent will not raise you when you lead on the flop. His likely game plan is to simply call you down if a third card to the flush comes on fourth street, and to raise on fourth street if a non-threatening card hits. This means that you can win $90 most of the time (bet-raise-reraise on fourth street), since it's about 4-1 against a spade hitting the board. If that spade comes, you'll probably be held to only a $50 win (assuming he doesn't complete a flush).

Of course, your opponent may hold only a couple of big cards, not an overpair. Even so, he may well decide to play the hand as if he had an overpair, at least until he finds out you've got a good hand. If you check-raise on the flop, he will probably call your raise, and release the hand on fourth street when you bet. If you lead, he may well raise you, and make a crying call on your reraise. That is $30 out of him already, with some chance to make more. Since you're checking on fourth street, he might pay you off when you bet on the end. He will pay you off for sure if he pairs, and he might even raise. All in all, I don't think betting on the flop will hurt you even if the opponent does not have an overpair.

Please don't read this article and think I am telling you to always bet right out when you flop a set, or have a probable winning hand. Rather, what you need to do is think about who your opponent is and what he may hold. If he is a regular in the game, you need to vary your play with big hands. The point is that poker is not a game where all the plays are semi-automatic. It is a game where the plays should be made as a result of thinking about what will work best in each individual situation. By tailoring your plays, you optimize your result.

THE RERAISE

The raise is an intimidating poker play; the reraise, even more so. To tell a player who raises the pot that he probably does not have the best hand seems to connote a monster holding. In certain games with unsophisticated players, it simply says, "I have the nuts."

Among top players in tough games, the reraise is often used as a tactical weapon. The reraiser has a good hand, to be sure, but it may well be a long way from a rockcrusher. Let us look at some ways a good player can use the reraise as a valuable tool.

One thing we can hope for with a reraise (as with a bet or a raise) is simply to win the pot. At big-bet poker, such as no-limit hold'em or pot-limit Omaha, we often are able to accomplish that goal. At limit play, which will be the setting for all the discussions in this article, such a hope is usually unrealistic. By the time you can reraise, there is usually so much money in the pot that your opponent will try to draw out, even if he gives you credit for the hand your bet represents.

Of course, a reraise gets more money into the pot. Sometimes this will be our chief aim. But here, we have a very good hand and are simply trying to extract the maximum. Naturally, you do not need to be a skillful player to employ a reraise in this fashion. So here we will be mainly looking at situations where it is unclear who has the best hand, but there is something of value we hope to achieve by reraising. Let's list some possible motives for reraising with a less than gargantuan hand:

(1) To narrow the field. Knocking out players is a worthwhile achievement any time the opponents are in striking distance of overtaking us. Here is a typical situation from limit hold'em. Suppose you are on the button with a pair of nines, and the person on your right opens for a raise. Is two nines the best hand? Only heaven knows. There is certainly a reasonable chance that they are good, because most players who are going to play a hand in late position will open with a raise if no one else has entered the pot. After all, there is the possibility that the pot can be won uncontested.

The most likely hand you are facing with those nines is two overcards, making you a small favorite in a close race. But the reason you reraise in this spot is not because your chest is bursting with pride in these nineballs. The main motive is to confront the two players in the blind with a double bet, considerably improving the chances of eliminating them from contention. There also is another reason to reraise here, as follows.

(2) To seize the initiative. This is especially important in a form of poker like hold'em, where a heads-up situation can easily result in both players failing to make a decent hand. At hold'em, especially against timid or tight players, pots are usually won by the person who shows the most preflop strength. After the flop, the reraiser bets, and his opponent plays only if he has helped his hand. Or the opponent makes a weak call on the flop, still praying for help, and releases his unimproved hand on fourth street.

(3) To save half a bet. In games where the limit doubles on the next betting round, it is often useful to act strongly on the cheap street. A classic example would be holding a four-straight or four-flush on fourth street in a seven-card stud game. The limit doubles on the next round. By reraising on fourth street, we accomplish two things: We get more money in the pot if we make our hand, and we give ourselves an opportunity to get a free card on the expensive street if we fail to improve.

Another example of this is at hold'em, where the betting limit on fourth street is usually double the limit on the flop. Suppose you have a drawing hand heads-up with position on your opponent. He bets, and you raise, hoping to save half a bet by intimidating him into checking on fourth street. Unfortunately, he reraises you. Most players simply go on the defensive here, calling the reraise and calling again on fourth street. Consider reraising him! The reraise has a good chance of accomplishing the same thing you were trying to do with your initial raise. Many players

THE RERAISE

will play back on the flop with top pair if they get raised with drawing cards on the board. But when you reraise their reraise, almost everybody will give you credit for a big hand.

(4) To make the opponent misjudge the nature of our hand. This may induce him to make an incorrect play. This happens a lot at lowball draw. We open in late position with a raise, holding a hand such as 9-6-3-2-A, and the big blind reraises. Against most players, I think it is right to reraise with this type of flexible hand. Often, you can make the opponent break his hand and draw a card; you, of course, will then stand pat and have the best of it. If your play does not dissuade him from standing pat, you draw a card. At least you are hitting to a six if your ploy fails to work.

These several reasons are only a few of the many uses of the reraise as a tactical weapon. The point is that most weaker players are simply driven into a shell if they get raised, unless they have a clearly superior hand. Think about reraising; it may well be the right play. The top players do it quite often. Even when the reraise fails to achieve its aim on a given deal, the overall result will be to give you an aggressive table image that will help get your really good hands paid off.

FOLLOW THROUGH

As I am writing this article, it is that wonderful time in the Spring when The Masters golf tournament is held (It is the precursor time-wise for the World Series Of Poker, another favorite springtime event.) Some of the golfers have really beautiful swings. One of the prettiest swings belongs to big Ernie Els, the young South African who won this event a couple of years ago. When Ernie hits the ball, his clubhead continues to travel in a big arc for a long time after contact. At the completion of his swing, he is facing the target, and he has brought the club so far around his body that it is actually pointing forward off toward the right at about a 45 degree angle. He has great follow-through.

Following through is important at all sports. The term means completing the motion you started in executing a swing or other movement. At poker, I like the term "follow-through" to describe continuing to bet once you have started to represent a certain holding. On balance, it is certainly a virtue. But unlike most of the physical sports, at poker you need judgment in when to apply follow-through and when to back off.

Here is a poker situation I have seen many times. The game is pot-limit Omaha high, my favorite form of poker. The flop comes down unpaired with a two-flush. Player A bets, and Player B calls. On fourth street the flush gets there (still no pair on the board). Now the original bettor Player A checks, Player B bets the pot, and Player A calls. The last card is a blank, so a flush is still the nuts. Player A checks again. Now Player B looks like he wants to bet, but he turns over his hand and sighs, "I missed." He had been drawing at a straight, and tried to steal the pot when the flush came. He was brave enough to bet several hundred on fourth street, but apparently had reached the limit of the amount of money he was willing to spend on a steal. When he got called on fourth street, he felt the jig was up, and did not want to invest in any more charading.

FOLLOW THROUGH

What usually happens at this point is that his opponent, Player B, turns over a set and takes the pot. Had player A bet on the last card instead of giving up, it is hard to see how the player with a set could have called. Naturally, Player B was able to call on the previous round, as he had a chance to fill up on the last card. But once that hope evaporated, he likely was done with it if his opponent bet again. Simply put, the lack of follow through on his bluff cost Player A the pot.

I'm sure if you asked Player A why he dogged it on the end, he would say something like this. "Of course, if I knew what my opponent had, I would have bet again. But he could have had a flush the way the betting went. He could even have been slowplaying the nut flush."

This is all true, of course. Betting on the end does not come with a surefire guarantee of success. But one thing I do not understand. When an opponent keeps checking and acting like he is scared, why do so many players give him credit for a big hand? The truth of the matter is that there are two reasons why the opponent does not figure to have a big hand.

First, there are a lot more bad hands than good hands. If you knew someone was an avid golfer, would you figure him for being a scratch player? He might be, but the odds say not likely. Talent doesn't come easy. Big hands are not routine to pick up.

Second, if the opponent held a big hand, there is a good chance that he would not have acted like he had a mediocre hand throughout the deal. Most players who hold the nuts will spring to life on fourth street, even if they had elected to slowplay it earlier in the betting. They want to put the hammer down, and either drive you out of the pot, or make you pay heavily for the privilege of continuing. They think—and sometimes say out loud—"The pot is big enough for me."

Follow-through is considered to be a needed virtue at big-bet poker, but it is also a virtue at limit poker. Bluffing plays an important role at limit play. To be sure, the fact that you can bet only a small portion of the pot means that your chance of success is much smaller than at pot-limit. But on the other hand, you are risking much less money in proportion to the amount to be won. If your bluff is going to get called three-quarters of the time, but you are betting only ten percent of the pot, it is obviously correct to bet, even though you are not so likely to be successful.

At limit poker, present-day betting structures have the stakes double at some point in the play. For example, at limit hold'em, the bet on fourth street is twice as big as the bet on the flop. So if you had deemed the circumstances right for a bluff-bet on the flop, and nobody raised you, there is a good chance you should fire off another barrel at the enemy.

The flop is the cheep street, and an opponent can call you there on a wide array of garbage that will not call another bet unless the hand improves. Of course, it could be that the opponent has a big hand, and is trying to trap you into making another bet; he wants the limit to double before revealing the strength of his hand. But as in pot-limit poker, this is not the most likely explanation of what is going on. The way to find out what is happening is simply to bet again.

Should you bet again after the last card if you were bluffing? You are getting even better pot odds at this point, with all the money in there from the previous betting rounds. Of course, so is your opponent. He is likely going to call you if he has anything at all. The policy I recommend for handling this situation is as follows. If the texture of the board provides a reasonable chance the opponent was on a draw, and you cannot beat even a busted draw, by all means fire again. There are few things in poker so annoying as dogging it on the last bet, and then finding out your opponent had nothing—but his "nothing" beats your **nothing**.

Note that if you have a hand such as A-K or a small pair, you actually have something. It is silly to bet on the end, because the large pot odds at limit poker means that any hand that can beat you is very likely to call your bet, and you can beat a busted draw. Save your "bluffs" for a hand that cannot win a showdown.

Does the preceding discussion mean that I am endorsing the concept that if you start out bluffing at the pot, you are always supposed to keep firing? Not at all. Some times you are supposed to take your foot off the gas pedal. Some reasons to back off would be if you get raised, you get multiple callers, a card comes on

FOLLOW THROUGH

fourth street that looks like it helped the enemy, or if you get looked up by a calling station that will stick to you like a fly to glue.

I am saying two things. First, it is my observation that many people get scared at the first sign of resistance and back off their betting prematurely. They worry about the opponent having a big hand when all he has ever done is check or call. Second, if you get called on the flop by one opponent and a card of no consequence comes on fourth street, it is quite likely right to have another go at the pot. The double-size bet prods a lot of opponents to fold on the expensive street.

It is not coincidence that the top poker players seem to be pushy bettors. They win a lot of pots with the worse hand, even at limit poker. Any time you can win a pot with a bluff that you were going to lose if you checked, this is a major swing, far greater than simply gaining or saving a bet. That is why having good follow-through is one of the signs of an expert player. It makes him a lot of extra money.

BETTING ON THE END

One place where I see a lot of limit poker players erring is by not being aggressive enough betting their hands on the end, after all the cards have been dealt. I can almost hear their thinking: "The pot is big enough for me, now let's see who has the best hand." If you bet into them or bet after they have checked to you, they will call without even thinking about it. During the hand they bet, trying to protect their hand and charge you a price for drawing, just like they are supposed to. But on the end, they act like it is no longer important to charge you any more money.

Players bet a wide variety of hands during a deal. They might be drawing themselves, or have a small pair combined with a draw. There is no reason why a stud player has to always have a matching card in the hole to pair his doorcard. There is no reason why a hold'em player should be automatically given credit for top pair just because he is carrying the betting. Lots of people—even you and I—sometimes bet a hand without having the requisite values. The other guy wants to see if you have what you are supposed to have. The pot odds at limit poker make it likely he will call if he can beat a stone-cold bluff. So when you have exactly what you are supposed to have for your betting, you are supposed to milk that opponent for another bet, to charge him a fee for keeping you honest. You do not need to have anything extra to bet, just the hand you have been representing that you had all along. Let's look at some specific situations and see how this idea translates into practice.

It is particularly important to bet a reasonable but not spectacular hand on the end when you are first to act. In fact, it may well be right to bet a hand that is even worse than "reasonable." Here is an example from seven-card stud. The game is $15-30 limit. The low-card opens with a forced bet of $5. A player with a jack showing raises to $15. You hold split aces and make it $30. All fold except the jack, who calls. Let us assume that neither of you catch what looks like help at any point in the deal.

BETTING ON THE END

You are high with the ace and bet throughout the hand. How long do you keep firing when failing to improve?

I have actually seen players take their foot off the gas pedal on sixth street, panicking because they have not made that very helpful second pair. This qualifies for a Caspar Milquetoast award for timidity. Your opponent will gratefully take a free card if he has not yet made the ups, and bet if he has. Naturally, you will call him with your aces. The net result is the opponent gets a free card when he has the worst hand, and you pay the same bet when he has you beat that you would have put into the pot had you bet yourself. This is not winning poker; this is wimp poker.

The real poker question is do you bet again on the end after you have bet out on sixth street? I say yes. A lot of the time the opponent will have you beaten by this time. So what? The principle is the same as on sixth street. If you check, he will (or should) know that you have once again busted out and failed to help those aces. He will bet his two pair, and you will have to pay him off, after showing weakness by checking. You lose one bet. If you bet on seventh street, he is certainly not going to raise you on jacks up. He will call, and you lose that same one bet. Where you gain is when you both fail to help. He is going to call you with those jacks! Yes, it will be a crying call, and his hand will already be cocked to flip those jacks into the muck. But his money will be in the pot, which is the part that interests you. Your opponent knows that there is eight bets (plus the antes and forced bet) in the pot, so he wants to make sure that you really have those aces. The year before last, you bet this way on a three-flush, and he still remembers. So he is going to keep you honest.

The same idea we have just looked at in stud also applies to hold'em (and other poker forms). Suppose you have a K-J in the big blind with a four-handed unraised pot. The flop comes K-9-3 of three different suits. You bet the flop and get one caller, the last player. On fourth street a blank comes, so of course you bet again, and he calls. On the last card another blank comes. You have a decent hand for your betting, but nothing extra. It is unbelievable how many players will dog it here. If the opponent bets, they certainly are going to call. It is sensible to bet yourself. Lets look at the pros and cons of the situation.

Betting gains whenever the opponent has a worse hand than you do, and will call (but would not bet himself if checked to). A hand slightly worse than yours is exactly what he figures to hold, is it not? He is unlikely to be drawing, because there was only a gutshot straight to draw to on the flop, and the opponent called again on fourth street. With a gutshot he would almost certainly have folded for your upper-limit bet. With a hand that beats you, it seems likely that he would have stuck in a raise at some point. (Had I been your opponent and held as much as a K-Q, the only question is whether you would have gotten popped on the flop or on fourth street.) Unless the last card paired him, or he is a total wimp, you have him beaten. The likely hands for him are either top pair with a weaker kicker, or second pair, something like an A-9. On those hands, he is praying to get a free showdown. Let him pray to heaven; there is no reason why you should be the one to answer his prayers.

There are two ways a check could conceivably gain. One of them is to induce a bluff. You are most unlikely to have the opponent bluff after you check in our scenario. He knows you have some kind of hand to be betting twice into a board with no reasonable-looking draw present. He knows if you were simply trying to steal the pot, you would be unlikely to check on the end. Therefore, he knows it is very likely you will call a bet by him on the end.

The other way your check could gain is if he was going to raise you. But as I pointed out earlier, if he had that good a hand, he almost surely would have made his move before the last card. If you do get raised, maybe he started with a suited king and that unlikely-looking last card hit his kicker. Maybe he is just plain nuts. The important thing is a raise is most unlikely, but getting called by a weaker hand is a strong possibility. Players who constantly fail to bet for fear they will get raised are too fearful to win much at the poker table. Sometimes you should take a small chance and buy stock instead of putting all your dough in a government-insured savings account. Poker is a percentage game, not an exact science. The percentage play is to bet on the end.

Had there been a draw on the board when the flop came, such as a two-flush, I think it is still right to bet. You will probably get called by the opponent if he has any pair, because he will be wondering if you had been pumping the pot on a draw. (You do sometimes bet a drawing hand strongly, don't you?) He wants to keep you honest, so charge him a fee to do so. Even though in this case there is a chance that a check will induce a bluff, once again betting appears to be the percentage play.

When you are the one who is last to act on the end, it is not as compelling a play to bet one more time. In our stud example of the unimproved aces, I have to admit that I would usually just show them down if the opponent checked to me. But at hold'em, I would bet that K-J on the end. I think the principle is if you are sub-minimum, just turn your hand over when the opponent checks. But if you have full values for your previous betting, you should try and milk another drop out of the cow. At limit poker, people call on the end if there is any conceivable way they could have a winner, because of the pot odds. So don't be afraid to charge them money to see if you really have what you are supposed to have; you do not need anything extra to bet again.

Since a bet no longer protects your hand when all the cards are out, the human nature tendency for many people with an ordinary hand is to simply show it down and see if it's good. You should resist this tendency and get the maximum out of the situation. Here are four reasons to push that hand all the way:

First, in most poker situations, regardless of the poker form being played, it is a good policy to assume your opponent who checks and calls is as weak as his passive betting sequence seems to indicate. Unless you are up against someone you know to be both tight and a habitual slow-player, the right play is to assume he is weak and act accordingly. Don't see ominous shadows that have not yet materialized. Wait until you have actually run into power betting before giving the enemy credit for being heavily armed. There are a lot more borderline hands than strong hands, so put him on the dog his betting portrays.

Second, money you get paid off with on the end is free money. That forty bucks he called with on fourth street was not pure profit for you equity-wise even if you had him beat, because he could have hit to beat you. Money called with after all the cards are out is a freebee for the winner.

Third, it is the nature of hold'em that quite often nobody has anything reasonable after the flop. Even in stud, that three-card royal flush can look pretty moldy by sixth street. Most experienced players will in heads-up situations bet straight draws and flush draws as if they have a strong made hand, hoping you will fold, until they find out your hand can take some heat. Therefore, when one of these birds hangs in there without ever betting or raising, he is unlikely to be drawing. He either is slowplaying a monster, or has a marginal made hand. And as we know, there are far more marginal hands than monsters, so percentage-wise you should put him on something mediocre.

Fourth, there is so much bluffing at hold'em (because of the aforementioned propensity in shorthanded pots for everyone to miss the flop), and at stud from players who are trying to pick up the antes and just keep coming, that the opponent who has any pair will call on the end in case you have been pumping the pot on high cards that never helped. These guys look at the pot, look at the big price a single bet offers on pot odds, and then look at you. If they have ever seen you bluff, you're getting paid off. You are probably getting paid off even if they don't ever remember seeing you bluff, just in case this is an exception to everything that they have observed so far. In fact, you will often get paid off when they are **sure** you have a hand, just so they can congratulate themselves on a correct read (as you pocket that extra dough). The only time you are not getting paid off is when you don't bet!

Lastly, there is no law that says **you** have to pay **them** off on those rare situations when you get check-raised on the end. Usually, your only chance in that spot is your opponent has misread his hand. Hey, pal, when you get check-raised after all the cards are out, your opponent has himself a hand. At stud, he figures to have trips or better. At hold'em, one pair is no good! Throw it away like it was A-K and never helped. People don't bluff on that sequence,

BETTING ON THE END

because when they have nothing on the end, and want to make a play for the pot, they simply bet their hand into you. They don't check, because there is no guarantee an opponent will bet and give them the chance to check-raise.

So the next time at hold'em you raise a pot and have an opponent check-and-call on the flop and again on fourth street, then knuckle it on the end, go ahead and bet a reasonably decent hand into him one more time. This is especially true when no ace or king is on the board, so the opponent thinks you might have A-K and never paired. Don't let the third flush-card intimidate you. Your opponent is unlikely to have a flush, and is even more unlikely to give **you** credit for having a flush. He's still going to pay you off— if you bet!

INTEGRATE YOUR GAME

I use the term "integrate" as meaning to make internally consistent. My dictionary gives one definition of integrate as, "To form into a more complete, harmonious, or coordinated entity, often by the addition or arrangement of parts or elements." Many poker players seem to use betting strategies that don't blend smoothly with each other. If you play against a different lineup every time you play poker, it is possible to get away with inharmonious betting strategies. If you play against many of the same faces on a regular basis—and most of us do—you are costing yourself money if your betting strategies don't coordinate properly. Let me explain.

Suppose my hold'em strategy calls for seeing a lot of flops. Obviously I'm going to miss improving most of the time. If I meekly throw my hand away when I fail to make a big hand, my overhead is going to be too high. I've seen hold'em players that are successful with a fairly loose preflop style, but they all have one thing in common. They make a lot of money by aggressively betting marginal hands. Second pair is not a great hold'em hand, but it is better than nothing. If the other guy thinks you are on a cold steal, he may lose several bets trying to run you down.

Suppose you are a conservative hold'em player who usually has a good hand when betting on the flop. This means when the flop is checked by all, you're not marked with a complete dog like an aggressive player would be. You should exploit this by stealing a lot of pots on fourth street when the flop is checked and a nothing card comes on fourth.

Here is a good poker rule to follow. Anytime you are generally conservative in early betting, you should compensate by being aggressive in later betting. The person who plays tight throughout the whole deal is simply playing bad poker.

Many people do not realize the wide variety in styles of the top players. Many times there is more than one way to play a hand and do well with it. Some top players are super-aggressive, like three-time World Champion Stu Ungar. Others, such as 1986

INTEGRATE YOUR GAME

World Champion Berry Johnston, are more restrained. One thing all top players have in common is they have a well-integrated style of play.

Let's talk about some players who do not have all elements of their game in harmony. I know an experienced pot-limit hold'em player who raises preflop and bets on the flop with a big pair, but turns conservative on fourth street. He checks there if he gets played with, to protect against a big hand being out against him. This peculiarity is not the worst part of his betting strategy. His terrible fault is he also checks on the end. After showing weakness on the previous round, he fails to bet for value on the final round! He could be making that fourth street check work for him by picking up extra money on the end. His betting strategy is not integrated.

Here is an example from seven-card stud. A lot of players are very aggressive in trying to pick up the ante money when having the high card on board. An ace showing is automatically worth a raise to them. It should be obvious if this thieving type of player is lucky enough to have two aces in that spot, he can usually get them paid off on the end. In other words, if he has bet them into an unthreatening board throughout the hand, he should normally go right ahead and bet them again on seventh street.

A common seven-card stud inferior betting strategy is always raising on fourth street when having a four-flush. "Always" is a bad word in the composition of a poker strategy. Whenever a habitual four-flush raiser fails to raise on fourth street when his upcards are suited, an alert opponent will realize that a third upcard on suit is not a legitimate threat. Vary your betting strategy so opponents are unsure of your holdings. In my opinion, any habit is a bad habit when it comes to poker betting patterns, because it implies always betting a certain type of hand the same way.

If you want to improve your poker results, examine your betting strategies. Are you exploiting the table image your early play creates? Hyper-aggression in early play creates the ability to make money value-betting marginal hands later. Conservatism in early play sets up steals in later betting. If you have the reputation for being the Rock of Gibraltar in a certain player's eyes, this is a license to hijack his eyeteeth. A thieving reputation sets up good value-bet situations that can't be exploited as well by someone with a conservative image.

If you follow my advice, you can get away with playing certain type hands in an unorthodox fashion if the follow-up is correct. Avoid inconsistencies. By coordinating all the elements of your betting strategy, the whole is considerably strengthened. Each action has a reaction. Every strategy in late-round betting should be keyed to your style of play in early betting. By integrating your game properly, you can maximize your poker profits.

SHORTHANDED POKER

Shorthanded poker calls for a major adjustment in player strategy from that used in a full game. The values for hands shift considerably, the type of hand you look for is different, and the campaign plan for how you play a hand puts a greater emphasis on aggressiveness.

Let's define what we mean by "shorthanded" before we go further. For a two-handed matchup we prefer the term "heads-up," so that is a separate category, though most of what is said here will still apply. Casino cardrooms usually lessen their rake for shorthanded games; their dividing line normally is to consider five players or less as "short," and six or more as "full." Since such divisions are somewhat arbitrary, let us use the term "shorthanded" to mean three to five players, and "full" to mean eight to ten players. Those games with five to seven players carry some of the strategy elements used for both a smaller and larger number of players.

Even though you may be one of those fraidy-cats that shuns shorthanded money games like the plague, it still will be helpful to know the proper strategy for shorthanded play. For one thing, any poker tournament entrant should be prepared to play shorthanded. The sliding scale used in tournament prize fund payoffs places far greater weight on the top few spots. You can't get to those spots without playing shorthanded poker for a while.

Many situations can arise in a full game that are quite similar to shorthanded play. For example, if you are on the button in a hold'em game, and all the other players fold around to you, there will only be the button and the blinds to contend for the pot. The hand values will not be exactly the same as if you had started with only three players, because the deck figures to be richer in high cards, particularly aces. But the type of hands you build and the way you play them will be the same as in a shorthanded game. So even if you don't enter tournaments, and go for a walk anytime there are less than seven players at the table, you still cannot escape the fact that you need to know how to adjust your game for shorthanded situations. It is one of those elements of poker that every player needs to know.

Naturally, you don't need as big a hand to beat two or three other people as you need to conquer a whole table. At seven-card stud, one big pair is often a winning hand. At hold'em, second pair may well be enough, and top pair no kicker is quite a good hand. So you have to upgrade the value attached to moderate hands that shouldn't be played at a full table.

You also need to make a major adjustment in the type of hands you build. At shorthanded play, drawing hands go down in value, and high cards go up in value. You don't need to make a big hand like a straight or flush to win the pot. In most forms of poker, you are not the favorite to complete a four-straight or four-flush. Often the price against that hand helping some time before the end will be close to 2-to-1 against. Since most pots in a shorthanded game get reduced to heads-up play rather quickly, you don't get a good price on a draw according to the pot odds.

At poker, what you build is what you usually get. Play a K-10 offsuit, and you are building a medium-to-large pair. Play a 7-6 suited, and you are building either a small pair or a draw. In a full game, these hands may be rather close in value—and seldom worth playing. At shorthanded play, the 7-6 suited is an even worse hand, but the K-10 is a reasonable holding. Keep the distinction in mind next time at hold'em you are on the button in either a full or shorthanded game, and everyone else folds in front of you. Throw those little connectors away, whether suited or unsuited. Raise with hands like K-J, K-10, A-10, and A-9. Maybe you can steal, and often it is the best hand.

The most important principle in shorthanded play is to be aggressive. When you do enter the arena, be prepared to fire those chips. Many times, the opponents will have nothing, or next to nothing. Even when he has you beaten, and fails to fold under fire, most of the time there will be a reasonable chance to draw out on him. He will seldom be so far in front as to be uncatchable.

It stands to reason that if you are lucky enough to make a big hand, and you are in with an aggressive player, it may be right

SHORTHANDED POKER

to slowplay. At shorthanded play, your opponent is less likely to be within range of drawing out, and more likely to ditch his hand if you apply any heat.

A nice feature of shorthanded play is that if there is a weak player in the game, you can get involved with him quite frequently. Naturally, the type of weak player you are looking for in a shorthanded game is the passive calling type, rather than the over-aggressive maniac. The overlay against a weak player in shorthanded play is greater than anything you can get in a full game.

We have really just scratched the surface of shorthanded strategy. But it should be obvious that every poker player needs to adjust his methods when there are less players involved. If you do not know how to play shorthanded, you are not maximizing your poker earnings.

TURNING PRO

There are a lot of social poker players who dream of becoming professional poker players. I think most people who have an enjoyable hobby or activity dream about how nice it would be if they could make a living at doing the thing that they love. This applies to everybody, whether their hobby is painting, golf, or a card game. But when we compare poker to the other aforementioned activities, we see a strong similarity.

Only a few people, the cream of the crop, are actually able to make the successful transition from amateur to professional status. For every artist that has a fine reputation and rakes in the big bucks, there are hundreds of would-be artists who seem to put out high-quality work, but make little or nothing by way of income. For every golfer on the pro tour, there are hordes of golfers that "only" need to take a few strokes off their score to make the big move.

At poker, a lot of people play well enough to make some extra pocket money, but few are able to earn a comfortable living. The reason is you not only need to show a profit; you must also cover your living expenses. And it is simply not possible to do this without moving up from those soft lowstakes games to the much tougher higher-limit games. I would say that a poker player must be able to play winning poker on a sustained basis in the $15-30 stakes level at the minimum to be able to earn enough money to cover that nut every month.

One of the reasons it is so hard to make a living at low-stakes poker, even for a frugal person, is the rake structure. The rake is not directly proportional to the size of the game. Even though you pay more to play in the higher-limit games, the ratio of rake to stakes is substantially less as the game size increases. For example, in the typical California cardroom, the rake for $10-20 limit is five dollars a half-hour per person, but for $20-40 limit, it is seven dollars per half-hour. Not until the $50-100 level does it double to ten dollars per half-hour. So it is possible to put in many hours and beat the heck out of a little game, and still not cover the rake and your living expenses.

If you can beat a small game on a steady basis, what is your chance of success in the bigger games? Unfortunately for the people with high aspirations, it is much tougher when you play for serious money. Let's see why.

Most low-stakes poker games are pretty loose affairs. A majority of pots are multihanded action. For this type of game, the fact is you don't need to have all-around poker skills to be a winning player. You can get by with only a couple of virtues; the ability to recognize a good hand, and the patience to wait for it.

There are two big changes in the character of the play as you move to the higher levels. First, the players are more disciplined. Most pots are heads-up or threehanded action. Second, the players are much more aggressive. It can seem like every time you have a marginal hand, somebody is betting as if he has a good hand, and you have a tough decision to make about whether to stay in the hunt. Wrong guesses are expensive.

One of the adjustments you need to make in your game to be a winner at the bigger games is in the hands you select to play. This applies to all the forms of poker. A lot of hands that look pretty good to successful lowstakes players need to be thrown away in the bigger games.

A well-known poker principle is that drawing hands need volume pots. For example, at hold'em, if you have a straight-draw or a flush-draw, you will be about a 2-1 underdog to make it. This means you have a minus expectation on such a hand in heads-up situations, and only a marginally positive expectation in threehanded pots. You really need at least fourhanded action to make a reasonable profit.

Furthermore, there is no guarantee that your starting hand will even develop into a full-fledged draw, needing only one card to make a complete hand. Suppose you are dealt a three-flush for a starting hand in a seven-card stud game. There are eight players dealt in, and only one card of your suit is showing in the other seven hands combined. This means your chance of having the hand develop into a four-flush on the next card is only 9 out of 42, or about three-and-a-half to one against you. If no other cards of your suit were showing, the chance improves to 10 out of 42, which still leaves you more than a three to one underdog.

Since the chance of developing even a draw with your starting hand is much against you, it is obvious that you must be able to get in cheaply to have a plus expectation. Even in a multihanded pot, you would much prefer your starting hand is able to get in cheaply for the first betting round when you are hoping to develop a draw. An unraised pot is practically a necessity. Yet at the higher limits, the vast majority of pots get popped at the start.

When you are in early position, or even middle position, the character of a pot has not yet been determined. Starting hands with drawing cards need multihanded action and unraised pots. In the bigger games, you do not have the reasonable expectation of multiway cheap action like you do in lowstakes poker.

Let's put this into concrete terms. In a hold'em game, when you pick up a hand like A-5 suited or J-10 suited, you do not hold the best hand if someone is in the pot ahead of you or there are a large number of players behind you yet to act. **If you do not have the best hand, you have a drawing hand.** These hands need to be folded in higher-limit games unless you are in late position and the pot is unraised. Furthermore, you need to have either nobody in yet, or at least a couple of players that have called the blind. One opponent is a bad number for your hand, especially if the call was up front.

Changing some of your ideas about what constitutes a good starting hand is only one of the many adjustments you need to make in your game if you want to earn a living at poker. There are plenty of other changes you must make to go from a successful lowstakes player to a successful highstakes player.

One of the most important things you need to do at higher-limit poker is steal your rightful share of pots. At lowstakes play, where the majority of pots are many-handed, it is hard to steal anything. My rule of thumb at limit poker is to not try any moves if there are four or more other people in the pot. Even with three opponents, it takes a special situation to bring out the thief in me. However, for heads-up and threehanded pots—relatively rare in cheaper games but the norm at higher limits—I'm a larcenous fellow. So are most of my opponents. We play by the "Bones Dictum," which says you cannot leave the money out in the middle of the table to rot.

I see a lot of players whose idea of a bluff is to be betting a straight-draw or a flush-draw. Hey, that's mighty brave. Of course, I'm being facetious. Naturally, you bet a drawing hand in a shorthanded pot. You also bet—and sometimes raise—in many other situations when you don't have anything to fall back on. You bet for reasons such as the enemy checked, or because you are acting first and expect to get robbed if you blink, or because it has been so long since you were in a pot the enemy actually may think you have a real hand, or because your opponent is busy ordering from the waiter. Sometimes you even bet because you are so used to putting chips into the pot when it is your turn that you did so without thinking this time. If this happens, please have the presence of mind not to say "Whoops."

Naturally, you aren't supposed to bet all the time. The opponent likes to win a pot once in a while, so don't be a complete pig. Just make sure you steal more than your fair share. Do unto others before they do unto you. That is how shorthanded pots are supposed to be handled. You've got to play the game. I remember a person watching a highstakes game who said to me, "All they do is bet, bet, bet; but the hands they show up with aren't that good." True, but if you are the opponent and do not have a decent hand, you are under a lot of pressure, and the bad hands outnumber the good ones.

Another difference between lowstakes and highstakes play is what sort of table image you should cultivate in order to make money. At lowstakes play, with its multihanded pots and looser action, you seldom bluff. When you bet, you have a good hand. And when you have a good hand, you generally want to get called. This means it is desirable at lowstakes play to have a loose and gambling image. At highstakes play, as I have explained, you are forced into betting without good cards so often that it would be a blessing if the opposition caved in whenever you bet. We already know that you need to have a strong hand to initially get involved in a pot. If an opponent jumped to the conclusion that because you did not enter many pots, you were a tight player, and hardly ever bluffed, this would be good news indeed.

There is actually a big distinction between playing tight and hardly ever bluffing. It is the same distinction as between hating to go to war and being unwilling to fight once the war has started. President Teddy Roosevelt was actually talking about poker when he uttered his famous quote, "Speak softly, but carry a big stick." A poker player must fight for the money when he does enter a pot.

I am happy whenever I find out that someone has decided he is going to automatically fold against me unless he has a good hand. At highstakes poker, it is valuable to have the image of a player who has "always gottem," so don't worry about getting the reputation of being a rock. A thief should never be worried about having the reputation of being an honest fellow.

Most people believe there a big difference between lowstakes and highstakes poker because, "At highstakes there is a much bigger intimidation factor, because you're playing for a lot more money." Actually, although there is a certain element of truth to this, I don't think the difference is as great as most people believe. The reason is that water seeks its own level. The people who play higher-limit poker as a general rule can afford the game they are playing in just as easily—if not more so—as the people who play low-limit poker. So I really don't think that a person who bets a hundred dollars in a $100-200 limit game feels much different about the amount of money involved than a player who bets ten dollars in a $10-20 game or a dollar in a $1-2 limit game. He is likely playing out of a bankroll that is ten or a hundred times bigger than those guys in the cheaper games.(That is why I feel government should not try to control the size of poker games.)

You can see that becoming a professional poker player is a committal step that requires good preparation. You wouldn't decide to become a doctor and expect to practice medicine without the proper schooling, would you? Well, there are a lot more doctors than professional poker players. You need a poker Ph. D. to be a pro, so get your schooling first!

TURNING PRO

Let me tell you how I went from being an amateur poker player to becoming a professional. The transition was so gradual, it is really not clear when I actually crossed the line. In the early seventies, I made about a quarter of my income from poker. By the middle seventies, I was playing two or three times a week, and poker had become at least half my income. In 1978 I took up no-limit hold'em, and in 1980 I moved from Detroit to Dallas so I could play that game every day. But when I moved, and clearly became a full-fledged professional player, I was already deriving the vast majority of my income from poker.

My story about turning pro in gradual stages is by no means unusual. In fact, I believe it to be the norm. Most of my pro pals have a similar story to tell. Few of us are the flamboyant type of gambler you see portrayed by Hollywood. We are prudent people who prefer to test the water with our big toe and then our foot rather than doing a swan dive. Because sometimes that water is freezing cold. So for all you would-be poker pros, I recommend following that old adage, "Look before you leap." Hey, the pool might even be empty.

Playing poker for a living is a good life for a few people. The rest struggle hard and usually bust out. The worst thing you can do is burn your bridges by a rash act such as quitting your job, expecting to earn a living because you have been beating lowstakes poker. To be a pro you must be able to beat a highstakes game. Unless you have already proved your ability to do this, please exercise caution. Otherwise, you are liable to get yourself into a financial hole before discovering you are not ready for the big leagues. Many people have made this error. Don't you!

BE A GOOD GAMBLER

Poker is a form of gambling. To be a successful poker player, you must also possess the qualities needed for being a successful gambler. If you claim to be a good poker player, but are constantly walking around with empty pockets, people won't believe you, even though you may be speaking the truth about your prowess. A broke lacks credibility.

Let us look at the ingredients needed for success at all form of gambling.

(1) Have an overlay. We use the word overlay to mean an edge, so you rate to win at the gambling activity at question. At poker you must have the necessary technical skill to be a favorite in the game. Unfortunately, having knowledge is far from being assured of winning.

(2) Be objective. Gambling is all about matching up properly. Even a scratch golfer needs a spot if he is going to compete against pros. But a ten or twenty handicap can be a winner when the bets are settled if he knows how to match up against the opposition. At poker, it is the same way. Your success will be measured by how you match up. Generally speaking, the higher the stakes, the tougher the players. So follow Murphy's Law. Keep moving up until you find the level of your incompetence—but don't stay there! Drop back to a game you can beat, and play in it long enough to get pumped up before trying the next rung on the ladder.

(3) Protect your bankroll. The old saying is, "It takes money to make money." You need to feel the same way about your gambling bankroll as a plumber does about his toolbox. Without proper tools, you can't do the job.

Bankroll care is often called "Money management." It consists of two main things. First, you must play in games you can afford. It is harder to win in a game if you are under money pressure. I have to confess that if a big game is attractive enough, I might jump into it. But playing too high on a sustained basis is quite another matter. If you have the right temperament it is okay to take a shot once in a while. But that shot is never with your whole bankroll, because nobody has a big enough overlay in a card game to justify the chance of being put out of action.

The second part of money management is to not blow off your bankroll on what should be peripheral activities. Most poker players are not that attracted to pure gambling games such as craps. But gaming activities they know are beatable are a different matter. The two most common lures for poker players are sports betting and the race track. I have friends that make a lot of money on sports and the horses. But the effort they put into it is immense. I'm talking about working twelve to fourteen hours a day and using sophisticated computer programs. Most poker players would actually be better off shooting craps than fooling with sports betting or horses or dogs. At least they would know for sure they had the worst of it, which makes it easier to pull up.

(4) Play your A-game. Siegbert Tarrasch, a world-class chessplayer, once said many years ago, "It is not enough to be a good player; you must also play well." He might well have been talking about poker players instead of chessplayers. Can you really play well enough to beat the game if you are sick, overtired, or emotionally upset? Do you really think Santa Claus is going to drop into your game at five o'clock in the morning? Won't the cardroom be open the next day? Go home, get a good night's sleep, and hope to get your money back when you're fit to play.

(5) Don't steam when you're stuck. By putting in some extra action on starting hands, such as a preflop raise in hold'em, it is possible to build a lot bigger pot. The next step is to try and steal it, since you don't have a legitimate hand. But big pots are hard to steal, so you probably are going to have to draw out. If you're lucky, steaming will get you even. More likely, you will dig yourself into a hole too deep to get out.

How do you control your emotions when the cards have turned against you? Here are some ideas. Keep score by the month, not by the session. Have pride in your game. Realize that a lot of people play good poker when in front, but their game degenerates when losing. Try to be the exception. Go for a short walk, wash your face, and carry a toothbrush and toothpaste in your handbag or fanny-pack when playing poker, so you can freshen up.

Should you set a loss limit? That depends on who you are. I don't, and never have. I've made comebacks from some pretty dismal spots. Sometimes it is easier to win if you are stuck, because the other players know what happened and may pay you off figuring you are a bit on tilt. (Naturally, you do not actually go on tilt.) I've also had some streaks of bad luck that never turned around. My feeling is a gambler should have enough emotional control to still play decently when losing. But many people would be better off packing it in when the going gets tough.

These five rules of gambling are essential for poker players. Without self-control, it doesn't matter how much theoretical knowledge you have. You are still a soft target.

THE MENTAL SIDE

It would be hard to find a human endeavor that the mental attitude of the participant assumes more importance than in gambling. Watch a person gambling, and you can learn a lot about his or her character. Some people are a pleasure to be with when they are winning; then become "Mr. Hyde" when losing. Some people know when to quit; others continue playing until forced to stop through exhaustion. Some people can continue to play skillfully even though Lady Luck has temporarily deserted them; others descend so far in quality of play that they become unrecognizable.

Dan Harrington, the 1995 World Champion, says, "My edge over a weaker player when we are both having good luck is not nearly as great as my edge over him when we are both having bad luck." How does a professional gambler keep his cool and hold together through a run of rotten luck? I do not think you can simply say that tough gamblers are more disciplined people than the rest of humanity. They often eat too much, smoke too much, and exercise too little. In short, they seem to have the same vices as the rest of us. But somehow, when it comes to gambling, they have learned to control their emotions, at least to a far greater degree than most people. Why is this?

I don't think that we can point to one main reason some poker players have acquired good self-control; there are many reasons. Here are a few important ones.

(1) Having more experience. When I was not yet three years old, I took my hands and cupped them around a bee. My parents had warned me that a bee can sting. I believed them, but did it anyway out of curiosity. Naturally, I got stung. This act of mine wasn't too bright, but it did have an upside. I had a lot more respect for bees than all those kids that listened to their parents and never got stung. I think it may be the same way with gamblers. Of course, at poker it takes a lot more than one

48

sting to make your hands behave. But most good gamblers were once bad gamblers. After many experiences at having your runaway emotions destroy your bankroll, you eventually learn how to keep discipline.

(2) **Knowing how to keep score.** You can keep score of your gambling results by the day, the week, the month, the year, or whatever. The longer view you take, the better you will do. Those gamblers that try hard to win every session do a lot of bad things. They play when they are tired and when the game is bad. They increase the stakes beyond the point where they're comfortable. And they make unsound plays simply to increase their swing. When things aren't going your way, what you need to tell yourself is this: "My luck will eventually turn around. In the meantime, I must make sure that I do not bury myself so deeply that a run of good luck will not get me out of the trap."

(3) **Taking pride in yourself.** I pride myself on being a good player. By definition, being a good player includes having your emotions under control. I would actually be *embarrassed* to have people see me go on tilt. Guard your reputation, and this will help you guard your bankroll.

(4) **Knowing yourself.** Some people can play a long session, far past their normal bedtime, and not have their play deteriorate that much. If the game is really juicy, they can play all night and make a big score. I can't do this. When I get tired, my play gets a lot worse. I'm liable to become the target that is holding the game together. So I do not play all-night sessions. On the other hand, I don't steam when stuck. (This is not to say I'm playing exactly the same as when in front; it just means not going on tilt.) Consequently, I do not set a limit on my losses and then quit. But I know a number of world-class players that feel the need of imposing an artificial rule on themselves and limit their loss to a certain amount. The important thing is doing what works for **you**.

MONEY MANAGEMENT

The term "money management" does not seem to have a single standard meaning. When a player blows his bankroll betting on football or horses or blackjack, he is accused of "poor money management." He might even be accused of that vice if he bought a home and subsequently ran short of operating capital. Some of my fellow pros like to humorously define money management as "Managing to come up with more money when you go broke." However, we will use the term here only in the sense of selecting an appropriate size poker game in proportion to one's bankroll.

Most of the poker literature on money management seems to be written either by marginal players or mathematicians. They put out tables showing how large a bankroll you need for each size game, but certain of their premises do not appear realistic to me. For example, they assume that losing all one's operating capital means giving up poker, putting your tail between your legs, heading back to the place you came from, and getting a job. It is a wonder any of us are able to play decent poker with such a horrible specter hanging over our head. If this fate awaited us, neither I nor most other pro players would be in action, because most of us go broke once in a while. Usually, it's temporary.

What happens when you go broke? Well, it's certainly undesirable, but it is not the end of your poker career, thank God. You can borrow some money, or get somebody to stake you, or even work at a poker tournament or two. My point is going broke is unpleasant, but not the infinitely bad event visualized by the slide rule boys that will doom you to wearing a tie around your neck forever. Your playing strategy should take this into consideration.

The money management advisors—who sometimes have about as little money as most sports-betting advisors—would have you playing three and six dollar limit until your bankroll was big enough to buy the Nevada State Bank. You could then move up to five and ten dollar limit. When your reserves are adequate to buy Fort Knox, you can then make the jump up to ten and twenty dollar limit. This is of course an exaggeration, but you see my point. Their theories don't match reality.

The truth of the situation is a person needs to have food, clothing, shelter, transportation, and entertainment. These basics are not provided to him by the state. They cost money. You can win almost every day at low-stakes poker and never have a bankroll or security. Living expenses will eat you up. Playing at a certain level is necessary to accumulate money. That level depends on your expenses and lifestyle. Most people need to play at least at the fifteen and thirty dollar level in order not to go broke to the overhead of living expenses.

The fact is that going broke is not tantamount to having to slash your wrists, and you must play for fairly high stakes in order to accumulate money over and above your living expenses, mean you must be willing to place a small bankroll in jeopardy. If you are a pro with your case thousand in your pocket, it is still right to play in a moderately large game, instead of playing for peanuts until you run your money up to a high level. Naturally, you don't play in a $15-$30 game against the Las Vegas All-Stars. You wait until the game looks good. Pretend you are a soldier with one hand grenade left. If the first enemy vehicle through the pass is a tank, stay out of sight. Keep your powder dry until an easier target appears.

Once you have a big enough bankroll to play $15-$30 limit comfortably, you can start paying attention to slide rule boys. You should manage a $5,000 or $10,000 or $20,000 bankroll with prudence and restraint. However, sometimes a high-stakes game will look really juicy. One of the biggest myths in poker is that the bigger stakes games are always tougher. They aren't. You rate a poker game far more by the number and caliber of the weak players then by the number and caliber of the strong players. I would love to sit down in a no-limit hold'em game with Johnny Chan, Chip Reese, Berry Johnston, Daniel Harrington, Doyle Brunson, Stu Ungar, and two Hollywood movie stars who were just learning hold'em. I'd dodge the good players unless I had a big hand, and play pots against the movie stars. If the game were higher than I could afford, I'd still play. However, I would not play my normal game. I wouldn't be gambling or bluffing as much. If a game is attractive, it means there are some loose players in it. The way you beat loose players is to play solid poker, and let the mathematics of the situation "do its thing."

I hope you will realize that my advice on money management, especially the part about being willing to play moderately high on a small bankroll, is only for **winning players**. If you are not a winning player, your best strategy is to play in as cheap a game as you can stand until you improve enough to move up in class.

MOVING UP IN CLASS

Most poker players get the urge from time to time to play in a bigger game than is their norm. Should you? Perhaps. A lot depends on how well you play and how attractive is the game.

The first requirement you need is money. How big does your bankroll need to be in order to play for higher stakes? Most poker writers advise players to have some kind of five-figure bankroll to play as high as $20-$40 limit. How you're supposed to acquire such a bankroll playing lowstakes poker is a bit unclear. I guess you should hit a jackpot.

These large bankroll requirements involve two assumptions. First, it is assumed the player is going to play at a certain size game on a regular basis. Second, it is assumed that if the player runs out of money he will then starve to death. In reality, both these assumptions are (hopefully) inaccurate. All I am talking about is taking a shot at a bigger game. For such a purpose I think $500 for a $10-$20 game or $1000 for a $20-$40 game are quite reasonable figures. If you can afford to lose that much and the game looks juicy, have a go at it.

What type of game should you look for? Here a lot of players err. They think a game where most of the pots are getting pounded with raises and reraises makes for an ideal game. The fact is a game with a fast tempo should be avoided by a player with a short bankroll. Instead, a good game for him is where players often limp in on the initial betting round, and then stick around to pay off your good hands. In a fast and wild game, the "shot-taker" will be under too much money pressure.

Suppose you find a higher-limit game that has two or three calling stations in it. Good; take a seat. Now how should you play?

An important factor is that most of the players will be unfamiliar with your style of play. They are likely to assume you are "one of the boys" (or "one of the girls") and play in the same loose, gambling style that most people play poker. But what you are actually going to do is abandon all those plays that are only marginally beneficial (or perhaps even long-run losers) in order to dramatically reduce the amount of fluctuation that occurs in your stack with standard play.

Let me use a concrete example. Suppose you are normally a $3-$6 hold 'em player and see a $10-$20 game with a couple of known donators and some other players who are not the regular crew. Surprisingly, there is no list for the game, so when a seat comes open you slither into it. Here is how to play:

(1) Do not defend your blind or try to steal the blinds on borderline hands.
(2) Do not raise the pot without at least A-Q or 9-9.
(3) Do not bet after the flop without having top pair or better, except perhaps to take one stab on the flop if the pot is short-handed and raggedy cards come.
(4) Do not call a raise cold unless you were going to raise the pot yourself.

Certain plays you should avoid like the plague. Perhaps the most important of these is to put a raiser on big cards rather than a pocket pair and play your modest-sized pair for the best hand. A lot can go wrong here. The opponent may have a pocket pair bigger than yours. He may make a higher pair on fourth or fifth street. He may have raised on something like 10♣-9♣ and have your pocket sevens beaten when the flop comes 9-4-2. Do not try to run down raisers on inadequate values and a prayer.

A person who plays hold'em as I have described would have certain problems after the enemy got wise to his game. He would get pushed around too much and not get his good hands paid off enough. But for a one-shot short session against mostly strangers, I think he is a solid favorite. If he loses, his losses should be manageable. And there is always the chance of holding some decent cards. By altering your play as I have described, you can take a chance and play a little higher than usual if the right opportunity presents itself.

At the beginning of 1989 I had a very lucky run of luck in the pot-limit Omaha games, winning over a hundred grand in the space of three months. The larger bankroll has enabled me to play in bigger games than had been my usual in the past. I wanted to broaden my poker education by playing in some very highstakes limit games.

My normal stakes for limit poker had always been in the $10-$20 to $50-$100 range. That year I played quite a bit of $75-$150, $100-$200, $150-$300, and $200-$400. Here are some of my experiences and impressions.

The three games that I played in limit form were seven-card stud, hold'em, and high-low split eight-or-better stud. More time was logged at high-low split than any of the other forms. This was not because I play it better, but because the games seemed to be a little easier.

The money fluctuation in those games was not nearly as great as I expected. My two biggest wins were $8,000 and $5,500, and my biggest loss—occurring several times—was only a couple of grand. Part of the reason for my being able to avoid a bad drubbing was the short session length, but another part was my general philosophy of play.

Higher-limit games are structured differently than medium-limit games. For example, a $15-$30 stud game uses a $2 ante per player. In a full eight-handed game, this is $16 per round, approximately the size of the **lower** betting limit. A $100-$200 game uses a $25 ante, so in an eight-handed game, the overhead is $200 per round, the size of the **upper** betting limit. In other words, for high-stakes limit play the ante structure is about twice as high in proportion to the betting limit. How should your play be modified in this light?

I think most players who try to move up in class modify their play too much when doing so. The ante is high enough to affect your mind adversely if you let it. At $200-$400 limit ($50 ante per hand), it is easy to ante off a grand or two before winning a pot of consequence. However, the pots run so big, it is also easy to get even from this kind of deficit. Perhaps some players loosen up their standards for starting requirements to help overcome the high ante structure. I did not.

My philosophy was and is that the high ante-structure should not affect the quality of your starting hands. To be sure, you have to raise the pot with hands that might only be worth a call at a different structure, especially in late position. However, I firmly believe you should not be calling with any hands that should be folded in a medium or low ante game.

How tough is the competition at high-limit play? The good players are very good; the best in the world. Some of the guys I played with were Johnny Chan, Yosh Nakano, Rod Pardee, Artie Cobb, Jack Keller, Tommy Fisher, and David Hayden. However, if the entire lineup was composed of this caliber player, there is no way that I, a newcomer to this type of game, would light in it. The games I played in usually had at least a couple of weak spots; they were beatable.

I believe it is a mistake to judge a game by the strong players in it. Frankly, if I never sat in a game that had one or more world-champion players, I wouldn't get to play much poker. The Omaha games that are my normal habitat always have some world-class players at the table.

I may take some liberties playing against weak players, but I like to have a good hand when tangling with the toughies. Who is there to be afraid of when you have wired aces? With proper "navigation," you will play most of your pots against the weaker players, because one of the things that makes them weak is they play in too many pots.

Strong players have a lot of moves. They always seem to be representing a hand stronger than the one you are looking at. I don't give an opponent credit for a big hand in heads-up pots just because his betting arm is constantly in motion. The hands I build can and do have to take some heat. In multihanded pots, the play is more straight-forward, and it is more likely the bulldozer really has a good hand.

In any poker game, you must feel comfortable at the table to play well. This includes having a suitable bankroll. The minimum buy-in for high-limit games is ten times the maximum bet—twice the size of most middle-limit games—but this still won't take you very far. I don't think you can feel comfortable at the table unless you can afford to lose a couple of buy-ins without too much pain.

When playing in a bigger game than your norm, it is probably wise to slightly modify your play to cut down on the big adverse swings. Don't get involved for big money in fighting over the antes. Give players credit for a decent hand when they raise on the first betting round, even though you know they may be stealing. When you are going to get involved in serious combat, be sure your weaponry is sufficiently suitable. Leave it to the champion players —and the losers—to do their dancing on the edge of the cliff.

LIMITING YOUR LOSSES

The conventional wisdom as applied to deciding how long to play in a game when losing is this: "Limit your losses, but don't limit your winnings." This so-called axiom is applied to both gambling in the pit (blackjack, craps, etc.) and gambling at poker. It is pure horse manure.

The most important question to ask yourself in any gambling situation should be, "Do I have an overlay?" If the answer is no, quit at once. If the answer is yes, keep playing. If you claim not to know the answer, I'll bet you are going uphill.

Different people react in different ways when they are losing, and a person does not always behave the same way every time. The classic heavy loser at the poker table plays too many hands, bluffs too much, and calls every time he is not board-locked. If the above description fits you when you are losing, by all means set a limit on your losses. In fact, it's possible that bridge or pinochle are far more suitable card games for you than poker. You are what we call a "steamer." A steamer is so hot and agitated that steam seems to stream out of his nose and ears. A lot of the money lost at the poker table comes from steamers.

Very few pros set a monetary point at which they quit a game. The only time I would impose a limit on myself is if the game were attractive but a little over my head. For example, if my bankroll were in the $30,000 to $50,000 range, I might try a couple of $5,000 shots at a $50 and $100 blind no-limit hold'em game with a soft lineup. Given the same size bankroll, I would **never** quit a $1,000 buy-in pot-limit Omaha game with a couple of "live ones" in it no matter how much I was losing, until I was too tired to play.

I believe it is often easier to do well in a game when you are losing. In other words, it is easier to go from $2,000 loser to $1,000 loser than it is to go from $1,000 winner to $2,000 winner. The reason is simple. When people see you are losing, they go out of their way to play pots with you. They seem to think everybody is a steamer. A loser who turns a big hand is more likely to get played with then a winner. It should go without saying that when losing you must exercise patience in waiting for such a hand.

The biggest "escape artist" in poker may well be Roger Moore. (That's Roger Moore the topflight professional poker player, not the actor who has played James Bond.) I once wrote in an article how he went from $180,000 loser to $40,000 winner in a poker game inside of an hour. Another time he went from $250,000 loser to $30,000 loser in a big pot-limit Omaha game. What do you think Mr. Moore's view is on setting a loss limit? If he does have a limit on losses, it must be at least half a million dollars!

Does Roger steam when he's losing? Well, he looks and acts like he does. He certainly is an ornery cuss when he's stuck. He slams his fist on the table and glowers at the dealers. However, he does not **play** like he's stuck. He sometimes puts in a little more action than normal, but it's a long way from being the steamer his table actions would indicate. Sooner or later he catches some hands and gets them paid off.

My own poker experience says I'd be a fool to quit a good game just because I started off a loser. For example, one day I dropped $8,300 in a $50 ante, $50 and $100 blind deuce-to-seven lowball game at the Horseshoe Casino. At one point in that game I was stuck over $13,000, but I made a comeback of sorts. When I finally got my name called for my favorite game of pot-limit Omaha, I quit the lowball game. I won about five grand at Omaha, and therefore escaped for the day with relatively minor injuries. If I had quit for the day at any point because I was losing heavily, I never would have made that comeback. This has happened countless times in my poker career.

We are all individuals. You're not me, and I'm not you. When I'm losing, I don't even do a Roger Moore steam act. I try to play the best poker I can. While I can't claim to be totally unaffected when losing heavily, I still have an overlay. If your game goes to pieces when you're losing, by all means quit. However, if you want to improve at poker, my advice is to learn how to play when you're stuck. In fact, a pro who can't control himself at the poker table when losing should probably go out and get a job.

LIMITING YOUR LOSSES

I think the reason most people steam is they want to go to bed with more money then they started the day. It is better to keep score by the week, month, or year. If you're not built that way, here is what to do. Whenever you are losing, say to yourself, "I have a good chance to get even if I don't get stuck too much. I must stay within striking distance so a run of cards will get me out. I can't afford to play inferior hands, or I'll get stuck too much to get even."

In my opinion, the people who really need to impose a limit on their losses are the ones who shouldn't be playing in the first place. As long as you have a plus expectation, why quit? A pre-imposed loss limit is an artificial crutch, and crutches are for cripples. I'll bet you can guess my opinion of a quota system where you set a limit on your winnings!

SIZING UP A STRANGER

Those of us who play poker in public cardrooms are confronted with competing against people we have never seen before. The clientele of such a place is constantly changing. Furthermore, there is normally a big turnover in player composition at a table, especially during late afternoon and early evening. The ability to size up an opponent quickly is a needed virtue for such an environment.

Many times during my poker career I have gotten involved in a big pot with an opponent that I knew little or nothing about. A critical decision needed to be made based on minimal information. In such circumstances, it greatly helps to be able to properly size up a stranger and make the right choice. I'm sure you readers have also been in this type of predicament a good bit of the time.

Let me warn you before we go further that the information I am going to give you does not have a money-back guarantee for accuracy. In a number of cases, it is based on stereotypes of certain groups of people, and there will be many exceptions, because individuals don't always behave in accordance with the group to which they belong.

I also might add that I don't wish to offend anybody. We all belong to certain groups, classified by age, sex, occupation, ethnic background, and so forth. Many of these groups are composed of people who have a pronounced style of play at poker, even though there will be plenty of exceptions to the norm. All I am trying to do is give certain information so you can make a percentage play when you get involved in a big pot with a stranger.

Certain groups of people are far more likely to bluff than others. For example, age has a big effect on the style favored. In poker, as in life, a person tends more toward conservatism as he gets older. Senior citizens are much less likely to be bluffing than youngsters.

Women bluff less than men. Perhaps they are more basically honest, or less adventurous. In the old days, women who

61

competed at games were accused of a lack of killer instinct. I am not prepared to say if this was a fair accusation back then, but I can certainly tell you this is not true of the modern female. At any rate, I tend to give a lady credit for whatever hand she is representing, especially in a no-limit game. Don't think Q-Q or even K-K is an automatic call at no-limit hold 'em when some lady reraises you before the flop.

I feel it is quite important to know how much poker experience an opponent may have, and how familiar he is with the form of poker being played. For example, the game of hold'em originated in the South. When you hear "Ah raise" it is more likely to come from the lips of an experienced hold'em player. During the 70's and much of the 80's, there was a good chance your opponent was a hold'em rookie if he sounded like he was from "New Yawk", or looked like his ancestral home was from the other side of the Pacific Rim. Frankly, the days when you could draw such a conclusion are gone. There is now a hold'em game every day at certain semi-private clubs in New York. On the tournament trail, it has become a frequent sight for an Oriental person to win a hold'em event.

Especially in cardrooms on the West Coast, you are going to play a lot of poker against Oriental players. Historically, these people have always been enthusiastic gamblers. I am not an anthropologist, and can only speculate on what cultural forces have been at work. But there is clearly such a thing as an Oriental style of play. These people have a willingness to take a chance. Furthermore, most of these players are both tricky and aggressive. Note that I am talking about both the men and the women. Such a player can be caught with an inferior-quality hand, but you will be under a lot of pressure to guess on each occasion whether this is presently the case.

Hold'em is now a truly international game. Perhaps the best indication of this is the fact that when I went to Katmandu in the summer of 1992, To help out starting a game at Casino Nepal, there already was a home game where the locals were playing pot-limit Omaha eight-or-better high-low split. Amazing, for an extremely poor country that did not even admit westerners until about 1950. It certainly is a changing world.

Anyone who has a large cash flow from an illegal source will have a different attitude toward money than the average person, and this will be reflected in the way they play poker. These people have trouble spending the money, so they fire it up at the poker table. Such a person loves to bluff. It is a bit embarrassing for the poker community to admit it, but some of the biggest drawing-cards in poker are bookmakers and smugglers.

In fact, anyone who has a lot of money is more likely to be a bluffer than your average player. Those businessmen and other people with a big legal source of cash are not far behind the illegals in firing it up when gambling. Certain occupations are noted for having a lot of cardplayers in their ranks. For example, all-night restaurant owners, bartenders, and junkyard operators are three occupations where there is a lot of poker being played.

The way a person dresses and the amount and type of jewelry worn can help you determine to which economic class a person belongs. Gaudy dressers seem to bluff a lot, and often call your bets on suspicion. On the other hand, a guy with not even a watch, dressed in jeans and a sweatshirt, can get me to fold pretty easily. That grand he bet me might mean a lot to him.

Sometimes a decision based on minimal information can be totally wrong. I remember one time about eight or nine years ago, playing in a good-sized pot-limit Omaha game at the Horseshoe Casino, I got involved in a big pot with a total stranger. I had to make a decision whether to call an all-in bet. I had a full house, but there were some possible bigger ones. I recalled that my friend Blacky Blackburn had paged this guy to play in our game by shouting across the room. It seemed to me that this fellow was likely to be a loose, gambling player. Why else would Blacky make such a big to-do about getting this character to sit down with us?

I called the bet. The man showed me the nuts. Subsequent play that day demonstrated that this was not a coincidence. That's all the fellow ever showed the rest of the session, if more than a Franklin was put into the pot. Afterwards, I asked Blacky, "How can you page a rock like that guy to sit down with us?" Blacky

SIZING UP A STRANGER

replied, "He's an old Army buddy of mine." Frankly, I've never quite forgiven Blacky for this incident.

As you can see, snap judgments may well be wrong. However, they are better than a wild guess. Minimal information is better than no information. Playing a person for playing like a member of the group to which he belongs is simply something that will have to do until you find out through actual experience how that individual really plays the game.

The poker stereotypes that I have been presenting to you are not mine alone. I consider most of these opinions to be widespread among poker players. A person who plays **counter** to his group's stereotype has good chances for success. I know more than one young fellow that wears loud clothes, gaudy jewelry, and a top hat with a feather in it, that earns a good living by peddling the nuts. His counterpart is that sweet-looking elderly lady who is looking to steal your eyeteeth. But they are **exceptions.**

Now that we have talked about judging a person as best we can by his or her appearance, let's discuss what to look for once combat has actually begun. The first thing I want to know is how experienced a player I'm facing. To do this I don't pay much attention to whether a person's hair is dark, gray, or white. Many people these days take up poker later on in life, sometimes after retirement. So age should not be considered a clear criterion of poker experience.

The first tip-off I'm up against a rookie often comes by the person showing unfamiliarity with the rules of poker or the particular form we're playing. If the dealer has to inform the player when it is his turn to act, how much the bet is, or that he needs to post the blind, that person is marked as a greenhorn immediately.

It is amazing how much you can tell about a person by the manner he puts chips into the pot. Are they stacked and cut quickly and cleanly? Then you're up against an experienced player (though not necessarily a good player). Are they dribbled in slowly one at a time or splashed in a poorly controlled manner? This smacks of a lack of experience.

A player who is inexperienced usually falls into a well-known mold. He plays too many starting hands, checks and calls a

64

lot, and needs a whopper to venture a bet himself. The best way to beat him is to simply play straightforwardly, betting your good hands and checking your bad ones. The opponent is a favorite to be holding some kind of doggy hand, usually reacting to your check by gratefully taking a free card. Don't be afraid to check a weak hand here.

The next thing I want to know about an unfamiliar opponent is whether he understands hand values. When he bets, calls, or raises, is he likely to show up with a hand he is supposed to be holding? Especially, I want to know whether I need to respect his raises.

Let's talk specifics. Suppose you are playing $15-$30 limit hold'em. Don't pay too much attention to what a player shows up with when he raises on or near the button. He may simply be trying to steal the blind. More important is what kind of hand he raises on in early or middle position. Can he be pretty much counted on to show up with big cards or a big pair, or does he get frisky with small pairs and middle-size connectors? This makes a big difference on whether you call his raise on hands such as A-J, K-Q, 7-7, and so forth. You shouldn't call a solid player with any of those hands, but you can't let a clown keep running you out of the pot.

A place where players diverge widely on values is when they make it "Three bets." A lot of players are simply looking to gamble, and do this on hands that I wouldn't even venture a single raise. Others play so solidly that they are going to show up with at least a pair of queens. Be sure the situation is such that the raiser is marked with a good hand, as it doesn't require a big hand to play back at someone who may be trying to steal your blind.

Don't think it is necessary to see what a player was actually holding to begin forming an opinion about his play. You should notice the frequency with which a player takes aggressive action. Hands good enough to bet or raise with don't grow on trees. You can often label a player as unsound simply on how often his betting represents having a good hand.

I always pay particular attention to how a person likes to play his really big hands. A lot of players habitually check such hands hoping for a check-raise. This poor poker trait lets you know that he does not have a big hand when he bets, which is certainly important information.

Does the player do anything abnormal in terms of mannerisms? If so, I want to know what it means when he does it. For example, if he reaches for chips before the betting gets to him, does that mean he is going to call, or is he trying to throw you a curve ball. Do not rely on what such an action usually means—this particular action is most often an attempt to stop the opponent from betting—when you can find out what it means for this particular player, which will be more reliable information.

There are of course many other things to watch for that space limitation prevents our discussing. The main thought I want to leave you with is to work on improving your ability to size up new opponents very quickly. It is important to be able to make accurate early judgments about people, because the nature of public cardroom poker is to constantly confront you with new faces. By the time you really have acquired really solid information about a person, they are gone and a new competitor is in their seat. Snap judgments at poker are not always accurate, but you still need to make them.

THE TRUTH ABOUT TELLS

A tell is a poker player's mannerism that conveys information to his opponents about the nature of his hand. There is quite a bit about tells in poker literature these days. But in my opinion, a lot of what you read is a bit misleading.

The two basic ways for gaining information about your opponent are watching his betting patterns and noticing his mannerisms. For betting patterns, you should notice how often he enters a pot, what kinds of hands he raises with, whether he has a tricky or straight-forward style, and many other such clues to his play. This type of information is available about everyone, and is far more important than picking up on some mannerism that reveals information. Particularly at limit poker (as opposed to pot-limit or no-limit play), picking up a tell on someone is frosting on the cake. Yes, tells can be helpful, but do not think the top players win far more money than you do because they notice things like Jimmy's nose turns bright crimson when he is bluffing, or Sally shakes like a leaf whenever she catches a big hand. Getting tells are worth something, but observing betting patterns is worth much more.

According to what could be termed "Classic tell theory," poker players always want to deceive their opponents. When they are weak, they stick out their chest and bet with the thump of authority. When they are strong, they put chips into the pot slowly and hesitantly. Therefore, you should play the opponent to hold exactly the opposite of what his degree of confidence suggests.

Naturally, there is an element of truth in this view of tells. People do have a bit of Hollywood in them, and with no other information, the "reverse act" will be true more often than not. But don't think this applies anything close to a hundred percent of the time, or is the automatic way to interpret a player's mannerism. Let us talk about the ways I think a player should be using tells.

(1) You need an idea of how experienced a poker player your opponent is. A beginner tends to be less artful about concealing

how he feels about the situation, so his behavior may well be in accordance with his actual feelings. It is the more experienced players who practice deceit. And the best players simply put the money into the pot without any mannerisms. The tougher the game, the fewer the tells available.

(2) There has been so much written about tells that sometimes a player will simply act in accordance with the nature of his hand, trying to fool you by acting natural. I remember Jack Straus telling me the story of how he hornswoggled a guy into calling him. A group of people were behind Jack watching the play in a no-limit hold'em game. When the last board-card came, Jack let out a loud expression of joy, holding his holecards up so all the people behind him could see them. Then he made a big bet, enough to put the player all-in. The guy simply did not believe Straus would act this way with a good hand, and called. Jack showed him the nuts and busted him. So much for the "always acts the reverse" theory.

(3) There is no such thing as a surefire key to decoding tells, where a certain tell always means the same thing, no matter who does it. For example, there is a pot-limit Omaha player I know that has shaky hands most of the time when he bets. I'll grant you that shaky hands usually come from the nervousness of holding a big hand—but it does not apply to this particular player. This guy shakes whether he is bluffing or has the nuts. Maybe he has some sort of nervous condition; I don't know. He likes to bluff a lot, so if you put him on a big hand when he shakes, he is going to successfully steal a lot of your dough. When you notice a mannerism, **you must see what it means for that particular player.** Do not go by generalities in categorizing tells, or you will make a lot of unnecessary mistakes.

(4) Any time you make a play that is based on what you think is a tell, you are departing from what you would normally do. You are not making the play that is the correct and sound play that usually applies to the situation. This is why I think tells are not as valuable as some others make them seem. Since poker plays based on tells are otherwise abnormal plays, if you are wrong it is going to cost you. An opponent's tell should mainly be used as assistance in a borderline situation where you have a tough guess to make. Since tells are far from being a hundred percent reliable, to let one stop you from making what would otherwise be a clearcut play is seldom wise at limit poker.

Let me give you an example of being deterred from one's normal play by a "tell," which was related to me by a friend who is one of my students. He picked up pocket aces, and reraised the pot after someone had opened with a raise. The flop came down raggedy, something like 9-6-2 of three different suits. He bet, and the man gave him a real crying call, muttering about the hand in an artificial way that was obviously feigned. On fourth street came a three, and my student checked, since he felt the opponent was "doing something." On the end he checked again, and won the showdown, never finding out what his opponent had. To me, checking those aces was misguided. Yes, maybe the man had three nines, and was putting on a broken wing act. But my friend should have bet. The fact was he allowed his opponent to talk him out of making his normal play, without the opponent ever doing anything with his chips to say that my friend did not have the best hand. And I will be frank with you. If I held those aces, even if my opponent gave me a crying raise, he would get paid off. I'm not going to let some dude run me off a pair of bullets at limit hold'em when we were heads-up before the flop, no matter which way his ears wiggle or what he says. Note that if the opponent would have really had those three nines, all he had to do was keep a poker face and my friend would have bet again. Don't you think he knew this?

This brings me to the final point I wish to make. A good bit of the time, your opponent knows what play you will make if he does not do something to talk you out of it. Like in the preceding hand, after you have reraised before the flop and bet on the flop, he is fully expecting you to bet again on fourth street. So when he opens his yapper, **he is simply trying to stop you from making your normal play.** Why not? He has nothing to lose. Many times, what someone thinks is a tell is only an attempt to change what will transpire if nothing unusual happens.

Here is a hand from the 1997 World Series Of Poker, where I had a tell on someone, and the manner in which it was exploited. I was playing in a pot-limit Omaha one-table satellite tournament. A player who was a stranger to me called the blind, and I raised the pot with A♥-K♦-Q♦-3♥. The fellow called me. The blinds were real high, and there was only enough money left for one bet the size of the pot. The flop came J♠-9♠-3♣, giving me only a pair of threes, and no cards of my suits, although I had three big kickers that I might pair to gave me a big two pair. My opponent checked, and I decided to move all-in, hoping for a fold, but having some outs in case I got called. As I started to reach for my chips, the man grabbed his chips like he was going to call. What should I do now?

Here was my reasoning. The man very likely grabbed his chips hoping to induce me to check. Why did he do that? If he had nothing, he likely wouldn't even bother to try and stop a bet, because he wouldn't really be gaining anything. A free card is of value only if you can hit something useful. And if he had a flush draw, he probably would have moved in on me initially. I figured he had some kind of straight draw, and that there was a good chance of my getting a crying call if I bet. I sure didn't want to get called, holding only a pair of threes, so I checked. Some little innocuous card came on fourth street, and he checked again. Now I moved in on him, figuring that he was unlikely to call on a draw with only one card to come. Sure enough, he thought for a moment or two and folded. I do not know for sure if my analysis of the situation was right, of course. But I did win the pot, and may not have if I had bet the flop. The moral of the story is that even when you pick up a tell that an opponent has a weakish hand, there is still no guarantee he will fold if you bet. So tells can be helpful, but they are not a substitute for sound poker or good judgment.

YOUR EYES

When you are both a professional poker player and a writer, deciding what information to part with is not always easy. Some things you prefer to keep to yourself so nobody can use them against you. This article is sensitive stuff, and many years went by before I decided to put this information into print. But here it is.

Where should a poker player be looking during a deal, and what should he or she be looking for? I do not recall ever reading anything about this in poker literature or discussing this subject with a fellow pro. So in here I'll simply tell you my own methods.

I think most players follow the natural route of watching the action as it develops around the table. Frankly, I on occasion look elsewhere. Sometimes I am "Looking where I shouldn't be looking," whether it is at a player who has already acted, an opposing player's holecards being lifted too high, or even a provocatively plunging neckline. (This last item is done only between hands, and of course does nothing for my poker game.)

It is desirable to wear a hat or visor to keep the glaring overhead lights out of your eyes. But it is even more important to shield your eyes from being viewed by the opposing players. Where I am looking is certainly not something one would wish the enemy to know, so I always wear a visor when playing poker.

The eyes need a focal point. You are supposed to see things beyond and around what is occurring at the focal point, but you still need to be looking someplace specific. My eyes are usually watching the opponent's hands.

Hands reveal a lot about the player. Is the opponent nervous or excited? Are chips being handled smoothly? You usually need to be watching a player's hands to see if he checked or bet. Most players can keep a poker face, but keeping "poker hands" can be more difficult.

The first thing the opponent's hands reveal is how much poker he has played. Chips dropped one at a time into the pot are a rookie's trademark. More experienced players either neatly cut chips into a stack or use a forward flick releasing all the chips being bet at the same moment. And some players cut chips smoothly most of the time but get fumbleitis when bluffing.

A few people have some sort of nervous condition and always have shaky-looking hands when they bet. But when a normal person bets with shaky hands, watch out! You'd think those hands were shaking because the person is running a bluff, but this is not the case at all. The nervousness caused by bluffing is easily suppressed by experienced players. Those shaky hands are caused by excitement; the excitement of having latched onto a big hand. So if the opponent bets with shaky hands, you better start shaking yourself.

The tempo with which a player bets is very revealing. How fast did those hands come into the pot? Each player must be watched to see what is his normal tempo. Only by knowing a player's normal speed can you detect when he is abnormally fast or slow. Abnormal quickness is quite revealing. I find quite often this speed means a player is trying to act strong when he is really weak. He may well be on a cold bluff. But you have to watch out, as certain players mimic this trait of the bluffer to get you to call. This is why you must watch a player over a period of time to correctly interpret his behavior.

If the player is calling quickly, especially when there's a double bet to him, there is a good chance he is on a flush-draw. With a made hand he would likely have to pause and consider whether or not he has the best hand. He would have to weigh the alternatives of folding or raising. But on a draw, especially the nut flush-draw, he can make a fast decision to call.

At hold'em or Omaha, if a two-flush is created on fourth street, the opponent's tempo in calling your bet can be very revealing. If he is slow, and you can sense this slowness is because the opponent was considering a fold, he cannot have picked up a draw. Any hand strong enough to call with on the flop must be an easy call with the additional aid of having picked up a flush-draw.

There are several occasions I can remember at pot-limit Omaha where I got a hesitant call on fourth street, checked on the end when a card completing a backdoor flush hit, and faced a big bet. I called every time, and am still waiting for someone to show up with a flush. Their bluff on fifth street was detected by their tempo on fourth street!

It is not always possible to know whether an opponent was strong or weak by his first hesitation. Here's an example. At limit hold'em I picked up the A♠-4♠ in the big blind. An aggressive player near the button raised preflop and both the little blind and I called (along with a couple of other players who folded immediately after the flop). The spread was a beauty for me; J♥-4♥-4♦, giving me trips. The little blind bet, I raised, and the original raiser made it three bets. The little blind called, I capped it, and both opponents called. On fourth street came the 3♥, making the third heart on board. the little blind checked, I checked, and the original raiser bet. Now the little blind hesitated quite a bit and called. I felt the original raiser was foolishly betting the same hand he started with (he was a player who habitually overplayed big pairs) and did not see how the players on my right could fail to raise if he had made a flush. I thought I still might be holding the best hand and therefore raised, knowing full well that even if someone did have a flush there was no way I was getting reraised, with that open pair on the board. The bettor folded.

When the little blind gave me a fast call I instantly realized that he had the flush after all, and his fourth street huddle was a result of his considering a raise, and not from thinking about folding. When he checked on the end after a neutral card came, I simply checked myself and showed down my loser. My opponent had the nut flush. Note that my fourth street raise cost nothing extra, because it won me a free showdown. I would have otherwise faced a bet on the end and had to call.

Here is a common situation at no-limit hold'em. You are in the big blind, and a group of limpers call preflop. The only person who is a candidate for calling a big raise is the first player into the pot. The other players almost surely would have raised the limper if they had a good hand. The only obstacle between you and an easy pickup of the pot is that first player. Wouldn't it be nice to know whether he was sandbagging with a big hand or had a marginal holding?

Here is how to get a read on his hand. As soon as the first player calls the blind, watch his eyes. Forget about everyone else. They don't matter, as a player who has a big pair is normally going to raise another player who entered the pot in early position. Is that first player following the action or resting his eyes? A player with a big pair almost always watches the action like a hungry hawk, hoping the pot will be raised so he can come back over the top. If the player does not scope out the action attentively, he does not have a big pair. He may still call a raise, but you are not going to get reraised. I have tried this pickup play on many occasions, and have only run into a big pair held by a disinterested limper four times in almost two decades. And each time the player relaxed for only a moment after calling and then started watching the action. So study his eyes, and pretty much ignore whether you have a good hand or a bad hand. Just see if the coast is clear for a steal. This is a good way to stay alive in a no-limit tournament when you're not catching any cards.

There is one time when it may be better to be watching the opponent's face instead of his hands. That is when the dealer is putting out a new board-card at hold'em or Omaha. Don't watch the card. You can do that later. Watch the opponent. You can often tell whether or not he liked the card. And don't be taken in by theatrics. A player who makes a disgusted look may be acting. Once again, you need to observe an opponent over a period of time to know whether his disgusted look really means sorrow or is feigned.

Is it ethical to try and get a look at another player's holecards? My standards are the same for poker as they are for any other card game or situation. If you can see an opponent's goodies without doing anything abnormal such as craning your neck or leaning, you are not doing anything wrong. (These same standards also apply for décolletage.)

"Protect your hand" is a well-known poker maxim. And it means more than just protecting it against being fouled. It is the player's responsibility to protect his hand so when he looks at his holecards nobody else can see them. If he fails to protect his hand, you are under no obligation to avert your eyes.

Perhaps the most important thing I can stress in this article is the importance of watching the opponents even though you have already folded—which hopefully will be the vast majority of the time. It is too simplistic to assume that because a player acts weak he is really strong. Yes, a majority of players are actors trying to throw you a curve ball. But some are not. Only by watching a player over a period of time and seeing what sort of hand he shows up with after a period of telltale mannerism can you reliably interpret that mannerism.

A lot of information is out there if you look in the right places. Using your eyes properly is the biggest source of that information. A poker player who doesn't let the opposition see his eyes but watches the opponents like a hawk has a big edge. Let the player with that edge be **you**.

DECEIVING OPPONENTS

Deception is an integral part of the game of poker. If the opponents always know what you have, they are going to play pretty well against you. It is essential that they be kept off balance to some degree. Furthermore, fooling the opposition is part of the fun that goes with playing the game.

There are four general principles of deception that I feel are very important:

(1) Deception usually means giving something up by playing a hand in a manner that is less than optimum. This seems obvious, but many players act as if they are unaware their deception is a concession. They make a lot of plays that are so unsound that they cost big bucks, instead of looking for ways to deceive that are relatively inexpensive.

(2) In deception, a little bit goes a long way. This may be considered a corollary of the first principle. Since we are doing something unsound, we don't want to do it too often. When you do something strange and it gets discovered, people will notice and remember. Last month—maybe last year—this guy capped the betting before the flop holding the 9♣–8♣. Most poker players make these cute plays too often, and as a result give up too much.

(3) Don't deliberately make a deceptive play that is almost surely not going to work. Even though we hope to make some extra money on our normal plays in the future as a result of our deceptive plays in the present, this is something that will take care of itself. My advertising budget is zero. When I make a cute play, I have some reason to think it will help me on the hand right now. Don't deliberately throw away money by making a move that you know will be unsuccessful, hoping to recoup later.

76

DECEIVING OPPONENTS

(4) When you run a bluff, it is helpful if the message conveyed by your bet is of a specific nature rather than a general one. Your bet should say more than, "I have you beat." It should say things like, "I have trips" or "I have a flush." For example, at seven-card stud, if a player who pairs his doorcard check-raises, the betting clearly states, "I have trips." He may or may not actually have three of a kind, but he is clearly representing that holding.

Now that we have talked a bit about theory, let's see how some of these ideas may be used in actual combat. Suppose you are playing in a $20-$40 limit hold'em game. What are some common situations where you can practice deception without giving up too much?

One idea you can use is that a raise doesn't cost much if you were going to play anyway. For example, suppose you hold 7♣–6♣. If you open in early position with a raise, this gives up a lot. Your hand was not even good enough to call. Furthermore, you are thinning out the field with a drawing hand that begs for multihanded action. With all those players behind you yet to act, someone may repop you. Yes, some deception is desirable, but putting in three bets heads-up before the flop on a piece of garbage is a bit expensive, don't you think?

On the other hand, suppose we have our 7♣–6♣ in the big blind, and three or four players limp in with a call. Now a raise does not give up nearly as much. We already have a multihanded pot, and the betting has indicated that none of our opponents has a high-quality hand, as evidenced by their failure to raise on the initial round.

It is of course true that the first play, opening with a raise, is the more deceptive play. But it is by far the more expensive play. Either play would accomplish your goal of varying your game and keeping the opposition off balance. Who do you think you are playing against; Harrington, Reece, and Chan? Few opponents will observe as precisely. In either situation, if the opponents discover your holding, a portion of them will hardly be paying attention. Most of the remainder are simply going to make a mental note "This player sometimes raises on hands like the 7♣–6♣." So you should make the deceptive play that is inexpensive.

Another type of deceptive play that costs very little is reraising when you were going to call anyway. Here is an example. Suppose you are in the big blind holding the Q♠–J♠. The player just to the right of the button opens the pot with a raise, and the remaining players fold. The raiser may have a good hand, but there is a reasonable chance he has a rather modest holding and is hoping to steal the blind money. Your hand is easily good enough to call the raise, although it is unlikely to be better than your opponent's holding. A reraise is not indicated on values, but this is a good spot for deception. Pop him back and see what happens. You may win some extra money, or you may even win a pot you would have otherwise lost. Showing aggression before the flop at hold'em often puts a player in position to win the pot after the flop.

Contrast the preceding play with a player who is on the button with the 9♠–7♠ facing a raise and a call, and elects to make it three bets. This kamikaze pilot has a hand that does not belong in the pot for one bet, let alone three bets. He is simply spending too much money in order to vary his game.

A good place to make a deceptive raise is when you have a mediocre hand and are heads-up having position on your opponent. Quite often, the money spent on a raise will obtain a free card for you, so the total amount spent will turn out to be the same as if you had simply called. And if you help, an extra bet is gained. On your lucky days, the opponent decides not to call the raise.

Here is an example from seven-card stud. You start with the K♠ as your doorcard and the A♠–K♣ in the hole, giving you split kings. On the first betting round of a $15-$30 game, a lady with the Q♣ showing raises the forced bet to $15. You reraise to $30 on your pair of kings and she calls. On fourth street you get the 8♦ and she catches the 6♦. You bet and she calls. On fifth street you receive the 2♥ for no help. She snags the 6♥ to make open sixes and bets into you. Apparently your opponent has the better hand at this point with queens and sixes. The normal-looking play is to call and hope to draw out. I believe this is a good spot for a deceptive raise. Your opponent is going to be worried that you have improved your hand and now have kings up. If that is your hand, she has only four cards in the deck with which to beat you. A fold by her is possible, but more likely she will cryingly call your raise and check to you on sixth street (assuming the very likely situation that she fails to improve). If you help, you will of course bet again. If you catch the usual blank, you have the option of checking. The total price of the hand will be the same for you. Instead of paying $30 on fifth street and $30 on sixth street, you will be paying $60 on fifth street and nothing on sixth street. You get a reputation for deceptive play, and it doesn't cost a thing; not a bad deal!

I think most poker players appreciate the value of deception. Their problem is they give up too much to achieve it. By avoiding the dual errors of making a tricky play with a hand that should be folded and making a tricky play too often, you can vary your game without much cost. Most players will give you action if they have ever seen you out of line, so there is no reason to pay big bucks to get played with. And maybe you do not want to get played with when you bet. A tight image is as exploitable as a loose image.

STEALING BLINDS AND ANTES

Perhaps the most common bluff in poker is the attempt to steal ante or blind money. The focus for this article is how to handle subsequent betting rounds when you have bluffed a raise on the initial betting round and gotten called. How do you follow up your bluff?

Your basic choices are to either fire another salvo to win the pot on the next round, or to check with the intention of folding if your opponent bets. (Checking and calling is not a consideration.)

Let us first look at a scenario from seven-card stud. Pretend you are playing fifteen and thirty dollar limit. The betting structure is a two-dollar ante and a five-dollar forced bet by the lowcard. Suppose you hold (K♠ 2♠) A♥ in middle position, and decide to raise the forced bet of five dollars to a total of fifteen dollars in the hope that your ace on board will enable you to steal the antes. You get called by a player with the 10♣ showing and everybody else folds. What should your game plan be on later betting streets?

Let us look at fourth street. Suppose you catch a blank such as the 7♥. What determines whether you bet or check? Naturally, your action is partly determined by who is in the pot with you, your present table image, and a number of such personal factors. In this problem-like scene (and any others I may construct), assume the opponent is a stranger in a newly started game. In other words, you are being asked what you should **normally** do, not what you should invariably do. What factors influence whether you fire again here?

If your opponent catches a card that does not appear to help his hand, you should bet again. If he catches a card that looks helpful such as a second club or a card adjacent in rank to his ten, check and be prepared to fold. The reason you bet if he catches a neutral card is mainly due to the possibility that he started with a drawing hand. A frequent type of starting hand is a three-flush or a three-straight in the first three cards. If that is the case here, your opponent now has a very weak hand. Most players will fold a drawing hand that does not help on fourth street, so you should bet to see if that is his holding here.

Suppose you bet on fourth street and get called. What determines if you bluff again? You can now assume your opponent started with a pair in the first three cards, since he would probably have folded a drawing hand that broke off on fourth street. If the opponent has not paired on board with the fifth card, it is usually right for you to bet again. The reason is the limit has doubled, so you have additional leverage to move him out. To check would be cowardly and ill-conceived. (Note that a prudent check may be indicated in a structure where the limit does not increase on fifth street, such as "One to four dollar limit.")

If you do not induce a fold on fifth street with a double-size bet, the chance of running him out of the pot has become poor. By calling on fifth street, your opponent has created sufficient pot odds for playing out the hand and has "announced" his intention of doing just that. It is probably right for you to slow down and check unless you are lucky enough to buy a scarecard. If he bets, you will have a decision to make whether to call or fold, and it could be right to throw in the towel.

To summarize, in seven-card stud you keep bluff-betting on fourth street into a mediocre board in case your opponent was drawing. You bet on fifth street in case the double-size bet can move him. Once you get called on fifth, resign yourself to the fact that the only real way to win now is to show him the best hand, unless you are lucky enough to hit an open pair on the next card.

At hold'em, if you open for a raise before the flop on a mediocre hand with the intention of stealing the blind money, it is usually right to keep bluffing against one or two opponents. You bet on the flop into an average nondescript board in case they have failed to help. If you are called, bet on fourth street in any game where you are now allowed to make a double-size bet. In other words, at five-and-ten dollar limit you keep bluffing, but at one-to-five dollar limit it might be right to check. A lot depends on whether you retain any interest in the pot. If you still have some interest in the pot, such as holding two overcards, it is quite

STEALING BLINDS AND ANTES

different from having no outs. The preceding is an over-simplification, of course.

You can see from this discussion that an early raise to steal ante or blind money is seldom a one-shot affair. It is often right to keep charging at the pot on subsequent betting rounds. For this reason, it is much better to run this bluff with sub-par values than to be on a complete steal. At seven-card stud, (Q♥ J♥) K♠ or (2♦ 2♥) K♠ are much better for ante steals than total garbage such as (2♦ 7♥) K♠. At hold'em, prefer to have Q♥-J♦ or A♠-9♦ instead of 8♦-5♥. Since you are not going to automatically steal whenever you are in late position and nobody but the forced bet or blinds have entered the pot, pick hands that can get lucky. Betting with an out is a very important part of proper bluffing strategy.

ADVERTISING

Bluffing is making a bet on a weak hand in the hope of stealing the pot, either on that betting round or a later one. Every top poker player makes use of bluffs. It is a maneuver integral to the nature of the game. Sometimes we get positioned in a precarious situation, and the only way of winning is to fire and hope our opponent retreats. Other times a bluff is prepared from the beginning of the deal.

Many players have a skewed perception of when to bluff. Their favorite motto is, "It pays to advertise." This slogan is put into practice by launching bluffs that have virtually no chance of success. They are right that a side benefit to bluffing is increasing your chance of getting good hands paid off in future pots. However, note that I said "side benefit." Obtaining a long-range payback should not be the main goal.

Too many players treat their chips as if they have a portion set aside for an advertising budget. This money is to be freely spent in the hope of regaining it later. I believe their view is just plain wrong, because it leads to trying bluffs that are not going to work, which is stupid poker. Perhaps a more apropos slogan for these big-spending players would be "It costs to advertise."

A good player decides to run a bluff because he is trying to win the pot, not with the primary goal of setting up a future play. You can have a net win on bluffs and **still** get good hands paid off. Poker often resembles real life. A poker player should consider himself president of a corporation. Each separate subdivision within the corporation needs to be cost-efficient and show some profit, even though not all can be equally effective monetarily. Your bluffing department needs to show a profit itself, in addition to aiding income from the premium-hand department. This is modern business theory and should also be considered modern poker theory.

I don't bluff unless there seems to be a decent chance the opposition will fold. Since my favorite form of poker is big-bet poker (pot-limit and no-limit play), most of my bluffs are going to be about the size of the pot or somewhat less. My usual criterion is if it looks like my opponent is better than even money to fold, I'll pop him. At limit play, you may be getting pot odds of 5-1, 10-1, or even higher. Obviously, you don't need to feel your opponent is a favorite to fold to make a bluff be mathematically sound. However, you should always feel a bluff is the correct percentage play in that spot.

Many of these big-budget advertisers have only one criterion for bluffing; they bet every time it looks like the only way to win the pot. In other words, they bet whenever they don't have anything, regardless of the prospect for success. When you realize the worst fault of the weak poker players is playing too many hands—and therefore winding up with an obvious loser quite often—they drop a considerable amount of money by poor judgment in bluffing. Their bluffs are too frequent and too mechanical.

The chance of a bluff succeeding depends on a number of factors. An important one is your table image; in other words, whether the target perceives you as someone likely to bluff. These stubborn advertisers who bluff all the time seem oblivious to their table image. Even if they have been caught speeding several times in a particular session, they still keep a heavy foot on the gas pedal. Please be aware of how others perceive you at that moment when considering a bluff.

You may be thinking at this point, "It sounds like Bob Ciaffone doesn't have a high opinion of bluffing". This is not true. I win a lot of money on bluffs, for several reasons:

(1) I play big-bet poker, where a bluff of course has a much better chance of success than at limit poker.

(2) I do not play very many starting hands at any form of poker. This causes many opponents to pin the adjective "tight" on me. Unlike most players, I do not feel being regarded as tight hurts me at the poker table. Quite the contrary; it works to my advantage. When I find an opponent regards me as a "nuts player," he is going to face a hijacking.

(3) My bluffs are consistent with the previous betting on a hand. I normally portray a holding that is a very likely one.

Usually, when I run a big bluff, I know within a second or two whether my bet is going to be successful. Some guys take ages to throw a hand away. Sometimes this is because they are really indecisive, and sometimes it is a smokescreen so I and the other players will not think it is easy to induce them to fold. At any rate, if they don't call quickly, they are unlikely to ever call. There is no reason to be nervous about success because you have just bet a grand with no hand. Unless you open your big mouth, a staller is in all probability going to abandon ship.

Bluffing is a fun part of poker. There is satisfaction in winning extra money that is obtained by clever play, instead of settling for only those pots that we are entitled to by holding the best hand. A successful bluff gives a player the feeling he earned the money. However, do not overwork a good thing. Bluff to win the pot. If advertising by running several bluffs early in the game regardless of the situation is your norm, the most likely result is simply to get yourself stuck. Having to come from behind will not enhance your chances for a successful session. Even worse is the possibility that fate will not deal you those strong hands that are now ripe for making money. Instead, some good bluffing situations will occur that can no longer be exploited because of your present "wild man" table image—which you paid so much to create!

USING LEVERAGE

This chapter will discuss leverage in bluffing. By leverage I mean the way your bet or raise can represent a far larger sum in the mind of the target than was actually wagered. Imagine yourself in a no-limit hold'em game. You lead out for $100 into a pot that size, and I call the $100 and raise $300 more. Your hand is Q♠-9♠ and the board is 10♥-9♥-9♦, so you have flopped three nines with a Queen kicker. You have a good hand, but I might be holding a better one. What should you do? If my raise of $300 is an all-in bet, you have an easy call. There are many hands that you can beat, and if I hold a better hand or outdraw you, it is only a $300 loss.

Suppose we alter the problem by increasing the size of our stacks. Give each of us about a thousand dollars left after the flop. Now you have another $600 that is in jeopardy, in addition to the $300 needed to call the raise itself. The decision has become more difficult. It is going to be hard to save that additional $600 if you call the $300.

In fact, most good players would feel a call should not be one of your options. There are many possible drawing hands I could hold, in spite of the board being paired, so you should either throw your hand away or go all-in for the $600 more. At any rate, there can now be a thousand dollars riding on your course of action.

I can sense you thinking, "It's still not that tough a problem; just play back for all your money, and if you're beat, you're beat." Well, I can make your decision on how to handle this $300 bet real tough. Suppose you and I are the chip leaders in a tournament, each of us having about $5000. There are three other finalists, but they are all on short money. The tournament winner gets a $10,000 entry into the World's Championship and $3,000 in cash, second place pays $2000 in cash, but third, fourth, and fifth places all get dinner for two at El Greasy Spoon. Are you still going to play back at me with all your money? It is a long, long way from $300 all-in, isn't it! There is no longer any obvious-looking play as to raise, call, or fold. You may well be thinking about the possibility of an unappetizing dinner, and losing out on a chance to win a million bucks. I certainly am!

This vignette was to dramatize the fact that any bet that is not all-in or on the end will have additional force beyond the amount wagered. The success of a bluff often comes from this added leverage.

An all-in bet is much more likely to be called than a bet made when there is money left to wager on subsequent betting rounds, because the leverage factor is absent. The caller knows exactly how much it is going to cost him to see all the cards. This is one reason why a good player should make sure he always has enough chips in front of him to see a hand through. Short stacks get called; large stacks can bluff.

Our scenario used a no-limit game, but the principle obviously applies to limit poker as well. In fact, since the target of the bet is usually getting sizable pot odds at limit poker, the leverage factor is usually needed to induce a fold. The target is not thinking, "How much did he bet?" but, "How much will this hand cost me if I see it through?"

Without leverage you are normally going to get called at limit poker if your opponent has anything. Therefore, you should not bluff after all the cards are out unless you are totally broke. Let me give you a concrete example. Suppose you raise the pot in a limit hold'em game and the flop comes 10♥-9♥-3♣. There is one caller, and then an offsuit deuce comes on fourth street. You bet again and get called. On the end comes an offsuit four, so it looks like nobody has helped his original hand. If you hold Q♥-J♥, by all means bet again. There are many better hands than yours that an opponent may fold.

Suppose you hold A♥-Q♥ on the same betting sequence. A lot of players also mechanically bet on the end with this type of hand, but I believe it is the wrong play. If your opponent has a pair, he is almost sure to call. If your opponent does not have a pair, he will almost surely fold. In other words, if you bet, it is very unlikely your opponent will misplay his hand, regardless what he holds. We call this ill-conceived type of bet where you only get called when you're beat and don't make any money when your hand is good, "The bet that can't be right."

There are many players who would bet an ace-queen in this situation. Their reasoning is, "My opponent may have been drawing, so if I check, and he bets, I am going to have to call. Since I'm going to call, I must bet." I do not agree with this logic. Sometimes checking and calling is the right play. In this situation just discussed, check-and-call is the only way to win an extra bet on the end if you have the best hand. (Yes, your opponents sometimes bluff). In addition to inducing a bluff, checking ace-queen on the end avoids the unfortunate situation where you bluff-bet and get raised by what may also be a bluff.

The main point to this discussion is how to handle situations where you have no leverage of the threatened additional loss. You should not bluff with weak hands, but only with no hand at all. This of course only applies to limit poker, where the opponent is getting an attractive price from the pot on a call.

YOUR TABLE IMAGE

Most players think the proper way to play poker is to promote the image of a loose player with a lot of gamble, but actually play tight cards. This is one way to play. It is by far the most common method. I think the main reason for this is most of us learn to play poker in home games, and only later start playing in public cardrooms. In a home game, you would like to be able to come back and get another load. A tight player is not a desirable opponent, and is in danger of getting barred. The natural tendency in this environment is to try and look like we are giving action.

There is another way to play the game when you are doing battle in a public cardroom. You can play tight, and use that table image to steal a pot here and there. This works doubly well for you. By not playing many hands, you are giving yourself a better chance of having the superior weapon when doing battle. The fact that you may go a while without playing a hand means that you will be labeled "tight," which will cause many of your opponents—incorrectly—to think you are reluctant to run bluffs.

I feel the important principle is to play the opposite of your table image. This can be done effectively with either method. You can appear loose and play tight, or appear tight and do some stealing. The second method has the advantage of aiming to win the whole pot instead of an extra bet or two. It also means you do not have to play unsound poker to create the desired image.

When I sit down in a poker game, I do not initially try to create a particular image. I just play the cards dealt to me. Some days I'll hold pretty good early in the game, and it will look to some people that I am playing loose, because I'm in quite a few pots. I know my image is that I am gambling a bit, so I'm less likely to attempt a bluff. Other days I will be in a mood to play aggressively, but Lady Luck fails to understand this. I'll seldom get a hand that's playable, let alone worth a raise. After an hour or two of folding, I will certainly attempt to steal a pot if an opportunity presents itself, and my image that day of a tight player will be helpful.

YOUR TABLE IMAGE

Let me tell you about an incident that occurred in the World Championship tournament. The game of course is no-limit hold'em. I have just been high-carded to a different table. The first hand I get dealt an A-10 suited, raise the pot, and win it uncontested. The second hand, I get dealt two nines, raise the pot, and again win it uncontested. (If you're wondering why I'm raising with those kind of hands, it is because we are playing with a one hundred dollar ante and a two and four hundred blind, so it pays to attack.) The third hand I raise the pot again, get moved in on for several thousand more by a stranger, and call. Bill Smith, the 1985 World Champion sitting on my right, smiled and teased, "Now we'll get to see what you've been raisin' those pots on." Tournament veteran Manning Briggs said astutely, "Oh no, you won't. He has a big hand this time!" Briggs was right; I turned over two kings. They held up.

The point to this story is that I played the cards that were dealt to me in a normal manner, but it looked like I was trying to run over the game. Some of my mannerisms and speech helped lend credence to this. Note that these extras are done when the deal is over, not when my opponent could be helped in guessing the nature of my hand. Also, the evidence is now gone. Manning knew that since I had created a table-image of an action player by my first two raises, I was increasing the chance of getting called on the third one, so I would be sure to have a very good hand for that raise, regardless of what I had previously held.

Cards run in streaks, so you will acquire a certain table image just playing normal poker. You should be constantly aware of how it looks like you are playing, and actually play the opposite. If it looks as if you are gambling, don't run any bluffs for a while. If it looks like you are playing very tight, by all means bluff if a reasonably attractive situation arises.

Many people feel that simply putting chips into the pot when bluffing is not enough. They slam the chips on the table, make comments such as, "I got you", and exude similar false arrogance. In Nevada, your opponents in public card rooms must be at least 21 years old. With rare exceptions, treating them like they were born quite recently will backfire. Fake bravado is easily seen through. When you bluff, bet with your normal betting motion and keep your mouth shut.

Another time to keep your lips sealed is after running a successful bluff. Some players like to show a bluff so they will get paid off later. This is precisely the kind of thinking I'm warning you against. Why tell the table what you are doing? The idea, "Advertise early and play tight later" is not the only way to play winning poker.

The less the opposition knows about your betting habits, the better. You might want to hijack this victim again some time. Besides, why is a player deliberately showing his bluff? It may well be with the plan of not running any more bluffs for a while. Don't be an advertiser, or get conned into falling for someone else's advertising.

Here is how "image" applies to me when playing my favorite game of pot-limit Omaha. Some people in my game—notably O'Neil Longson and Garland Walters—have the image of a loose gambling player who likes to steal a lot of pots. Their reputation is earned. They both do a lot of betting, raising and bluffing. This enables them to get very good value when they turn a big hand. Their style of play works—for them. If I tried to play that way, I'd probably have to deal poker for a living. If you tried to play that way, chances are you wouldn't have much success either. It's a tough way to go, and you definitely need a talent for it.

The approach used by a normal, sane, ordinary human being like myself is quite different. I don't try to cultivate any particular image—certainly not by playing a hand differently from how I think it ought to be played. Once in a while, I might **talk** in a certain way to foster an image that might make me some money. However, it would be a rare situation where I'd actually say to myself, "This hand is only worth a call, but I'm going to raise in order to promote a loose image." That's not my approach.

To understand my philosophy about image, let's look at a typical Omaha game. There are usually a lot of regulars. People such as Berry Johnston, Russ Hamilton, Blacky Blackburn, O'Neil Longson, and Fred David have literally played hundreds of sessions with me. I'll be damned if I'll spend even one grocery dollar trying to foster a particular image with any of these people. They already know how I play Omaha; making a few loose plays in tonight's game will not make them reassess my style and classify me as a loose, gambling player.

These guys are not my targets, anyway. They are tough players who are only to be gambled with out of necessity. The person I want to tangle with is that "live" tourist who plays a lot of hands and doesn't feel like folding very often. He is the person who I'm going to gear my play to, because his money is easier to get. How can I do that?

The way is to get him to put money into the pot when he should throw his hand away. Should I play a lot of hands in a loose, gambling manner so he will call me when I do have a good hand? This method doesn't work for me. All it does is get me loser in the game.

Fortunately, I don't need to change my normal methods in order to achieve my goal. Here is why. At pot-limit Omaha, an average player might play one hand out of three, and raise one hand out of twenty. I play perhaps one hand out of six, but I raise on over half the hands I play. The normal psychological tendency of people is to not notice much whether you call or fold, but to be very aware of your raises. To the casual eye, I look like a gambler who enjoys fast action because of all these raises. I also bet a lot of flops, which also helps my gambler image. Calling is an unobtrusive play. Betting and raising are acts that your opponents will notice, because they have to put extra chips into the pot on account of it.

However, the important thing to note is I do this betting and raising **because I think it is the right play on my hand for this situation**, not because I am going out of my way to create a loose image. My hands are generally of higher quality than my opponents hands, so I would like us to put more money into the pot. Or maybe I'm simply trying to get those chips into my stack before they rot out there.

What should your approach be? For most people, I think my style will work better than Garland's. To play like him, you need a super feel for what to do in tough situations. (You also need a big bankroll.) Most of us have to play a more mundane brand of poker.

In a nutshell, here is my advice. Talk as loose a game as you please, but don't play loose to create an image. If you have the correct fundamental approach to the game, you will look enough like a gambling player in the normal course of playing your hands without having to do anything special to show that you can give some action. To me, promoting a loose image by playing a lot of hands will only do one thing--get you stuck. Once you're stuck, it might not be so easy to toughen up and garner in the results of your advertising. The best poker advice I have ever heard is, "Play only a few hands, but play them strongly." My philosophy of how to deal with the question of table image fits like a glove with the way I actually want to play the game. It is better to just play good poker, and let your image take care of itself.

SHOULD I BLUFF?

The game is pot-limit Omaha, with a $5-$10-$10 blind. I pick up A♣–A♥–J♥–9♠, open for a $50 raise, and get two callers. The flop is delightful: A♦–10♣–6♣, giving me three aces. The first player checks. I am second to act, and bet $150. Surprisingly, both players call. The fourth street card is the K♥, making a possible ace-high straight. The first player springs to life with a $500 bet. I call, and the man behind me folds. The last card unfortunately does not pair the board. It is the 8♣, making a three-flush showing. (The board now reads A♦-10♣-6♣-K♥-8♣.) My opponent checks. I have the lone ace of clubs, and another $800 left. Should I bet it, or just show down my three aces?

My opponent has represented a straight by betting the pot on fourth street, and it certainly looks like he's not lying. My three aces don't figure to be any better than two deuces in this spot. The question is whether I should bluff and represent the nut flush, or give up on the hand.

Here are some of the factors to weigh:

(1) What does my opponent think that I hold?
(2) What sort of person is he?
(3) Can I bet enough for him to consider folding?
(4) Can I gain any information that will help my decision?

Let us discuss each of these questions. I had also raised both the previous pots. In each, there was one caller, and I won the pot by betting the flop. This is relevant, as one of my concerns is my opponent will be suspicious that I have three aces because I had opened the pot with a raise. The raiser in a pot-limit Omaha often has a pair of aces in the pocket. It so happens that I have had pocket aces three times in a row, but nobody at the table is aware of this. To them, I look like a player who likes to raise a lot of pots. (By the way, I hardly ever hold pocket aces on three consecutive hands, and often limp at pot-limit Omaha when I do hold them, so the present situation is truly rare.) My opponent is not going to necessarily place me with three aces in this pot. He probably thinks I'm nut-flushing, and is cursing Lady Luck for that club on the end.

The next question is, "Who is my opponent?" This is the first time I have ever seen the man, to the best of my memory. I have only been playing in the game for about fifteen minutes. Even so, I have formed some impressions of him. There are two factors in my favor. The fellow has hardly played any hands, and his clothes are not flashy. He is not wearing any jewelry, and therefore does not present the appearance of a wealthy man.

The fact that he is unknown to me does not necessarily mean that he is a loose and weak poker player. The game is a thousand-dollar buy-in game, and newcomers often turn out to be tight, solid players.

At this point, there is about $1,600 in the pot. It would be better if I had several hundred dollars more to shove at him, but an $800 bet is at least enough so the man doesn't figure to shrug his shoulders and give me an automatic call.

I decide to assemble my chips and stack them neatly before betting. As I am doing this, my opponent picks up his cash, as if anticipating my bet. How should this move be interpreted?

I have seen this move many times in my poker career. Once in a while, it simply means that you are going to get called. Much more often, this action shows fear. It doesn't necessarily guarantee that you won't get called, but it does indicate that the opponent would prefer you didn't bet.

I don't know whether my play will work, but it certainly looks right to put that $800 into the pot and see what happens. I stick the money in, and my opponent goes into deep thought. At least, his fingering the cash didn't mean a fast call; it showed fear. My opponent agonizes for a while. Finally, he shows me the queen-jack that I knew he had. To my surprise, they are queen and jack of clubs! He made a flush on the end. I had thought that he held only a straight. This looks like too much hand for him to fold. However, he gives me credit for the nut flush and mucks his cards. Despite the fact that the opposing player had a bigger hand than the betting had indicated to that point, My bluff has won a $1,600 pot.

SHOULD I BLUFF

These are some of the things a player should think about when deciding whether to run a bluff. Actually, at the table, I knew on fourth street that I would probably bet if a club came on the end and my opponent checked. The man reaching for his chips while I was readying my bet certainly did nothing to dissuade me. It simply confirmed my feeling that a bet was in order. In unclear situations, I usually put the money in and hope!

PICKING OFF A BLUFF

This article talks about the necessary poker skill of knowing when the other guy is bluffing. I am not talking about mannerisms, but rather the logic of the situation based on your hand and the preceding play. Most of your poker decisions about whether your opponent is bluffing will be made on factors other than tells. Making frequent attempts to pick off a bluff is not recommended, because most of the time your betting opponent has a real hand, but neither should you always fold when someone represents a superior holding.

When I first started to play pot-limit hold'em, I would fold nearly all the time somebody showed strength. I believe when learning a new game you should err on the side of caution. While this helped keep me out of serious trouble, it also encouraged people who played with me on a regular basis to put pressure on me. I soon learned that I had to call on suspicion some of the time to keep from getting run over.

Who you are up against, whether he is winning or losing in the game, the mood he is in, his betting habits, and any tells he might have when betting are all useful in determining whether to call a bet representing something stronger than you yourself possess. However, this article will only deal with certain situations that arise. All of the personal factors will be ignored in our discussion. Simply pretend you are up against an experienced player that sometimes bluffs. What are the indicators telling us whether to call or fold?

The first question you should ask yourself when facing a bet after all the cards are out is, "Does my opponent have something he could have shown down?" Most bluffs are launched out of desperation. A player has missed his draw, and has absolutely nothing to show down. He knows his only chance to win the pot is to bluff you out. Seldom will a player with a made hand pretend his holding to be even better than it actually is. The

PICKING OFF A BLUFF

tendency of such a player is to want a free showdown with his hand and hope that you were drawing.

Another question that you should ask is, "What does my opponent think I hold?" If there is a reasonable possibility you have a weak hand or have missed a draw yourself, there is a strong incentive for him to try a bluff. On the other hand, if you have never shown any weakness and appear to have a made hand, only a very rash person would try and make you lay it down.

Here are two situations where the opponent's bet represents a better hand than your own. Decide whether it is likely or unlikely he is bluffing.

(1) No-limit hold'em. You hold A♠-K♠ and open with a raise to $100 from middle position in a $5-$10-$25 blind game, and the two blinds call. The flop comes A♥-A♦-Q♠. The opponents check, you bet $300, and a player calls. On fourth street comes the 6♣, he checks, and you bet your three aces again. Your opponent calls the $600 bet. At the river comes the 4♣, a harmless-looking card. To your surprise, the opponent sets you all-in for $2,000, slightly more than the size of the pot. What do you do?

ANSWER — Your opponent flopped a full house and has played it in an unorthodox manner hoping to trap you. He obviously holds A-Q or Q-Q. There are several factors that point to this. First, your opponent has a good hand. He called two barrels by the raiser with a pair of aces on board. If he has a good hand, it is unlikely he would bluff. For example, if he has A-J, it seems like his best play would be to check and call. After all, you could be bluffing, so why would he take you out of the lead? Second, whenever a player shows weakness in the early betting and then springs to life with a big bet, it is much more likely that he has been "playing possum" than has decided to launch a desperate bluff. A good rule of thumb is when a player has played a hand in an inconsistent manner, his latest action is more likely to reveal his real holding. This is especially true when there is a three-straight, three-flush, or pair

98

that has come on the flop. Having a complete hand offers more safety in the allowing of free cards.

The final clue is what sort of holding he can put you on. Even though you have a good hand, it is a holding that contains no surprise for anybody. It is quite reasonable for a player who raises a pot and fires two barrels with a pair of aces on the board to show up with A-K. Even though you do not necessarily have to hold this hand, the opponent certainly ought to be prepared for it. Here, the chances are he is hoping you have A-K. There must be something better to do with two grand than wasting it here.

(2) Pot-limit Omaha. You are on the button with 10♥-10♦-6♥-6♦. The flop comes down Q♠-J♠-7♣, and everybody checks. The 6♣ comes on fourth street, making a second club on the board, and giving you three sixes. Everyone in front checks and you bet the pot. The player in first position calls and the rest of the field folds. On the end comes the 9♠, making three spades to a flush and several possible straights on the board. Your opponent bets the size of the pot. With this layout of cards, the only thing your three sixes can beat is a bluff. Should you gamble a call?

ANSWER — This is a good spot to pick off a bluff, for these reasons:
(a) Your opponent is marked with a drawing hand on fourth street by the betting.
(b) There were many drawing hands he could hold that did not get there on the end.
(c) The opponent has some reason to think you were on a draw that may have missed.
(d) Your pair of tens cut down somewhat on the straight possibilities.
(e) It is quite possible that your opponent would have checked, or bet less than the size of the pot on the end, if he had made a straight, since there is a potential flush on board.

PICKING OFF A BLUFF

(f) The flush that hit was the two-flush that came on the flop, when everyone checked. The backdoor flush would have been more dangerous.

Most decisions on whether to call a bet on the end with a relatively weak hand are based on considerations of the type discussed by these two examples, rather than mannerisms. Naturally, there are certain people who could not get a call out of me on suspicion, because they bluff so rarely. Other players bluff so ridiculously often they must be paid off. Not everybody follows the sensible behavior patterns we have been discussing. But if the opponent is a normal player, the factors we have discussed here play an important part in a difficult decision on whether to call or fold. Furthermore, the tougher the game, the less information is available by way of tells, and the more often you must make a decision using analysis of the nature talked about in this article.

20 PRINCIPLES OF BLUFFING

(1) Do not bluff to advertise; bluff because it looks like the right play in that spot.

(2) If you play only the type of starting hands that you are supposed to, you will have a tight image. This means your bluffs have a greater chance of success, so make that image work for you.

(3) The most important factor governing the decision to launch a bluff is the number of opponents in the pot. Against one or two opponents, bluff frequently. Against three opponents, bluff much less often. Against more than three opponents, it is likely to be a giveaway of your hard-earned money.

(4) Although it is possible to have a bluff work after an opponent has shown strength, you are much more likely to be successful if your opponents have shown weakness.

(5) When an opponent has acted weak, he is a big favorite to actually be weak. First, good hands are much easier to come by than bad hands. Second, even if he has a good hand, he might have bet it like a good hand, instead of slowplaying it.

(6) At limit poker, in most structures, the limit doubles. If you bet at the lower limit, if nothing special happens, it is likely right to fire again after the limit doubles.

(7) At limit poker, your bet or raise is only a fraction of the pot size. To be correct, a bluff does not need to be likely to work. Your guideline should be if there is any reasonable chance of success, not whether you are an odds-on favorite to be successful.

(8) On the end, you can bluff if you have nothing, but try to win a showdown if you have enough to beat a busted draw. An example is an unimproved A-K in a hold'em game, which should hardly ever bet on the end at limit poker.

(9) On a scale of 0 to 10 in poker skill, the bluff is best aimed at the player who is in the 4 to 8 range. The top players might play back at you if they are suspicious, and the bad players call you to see what beat them. Poker has similarities to warfare. You do not want to waste your ammunition firing at either exceptionally well-defended positions or worthless targets.

(10) A bluff representing a specific hand (such as a flush or full house) has a greater chance of success than a bluff that simply shows strength.

(11) The most effective bluff is one that not only says you have a better hand than the opponent, but also says he has little chance of improving to beat you.

(12) A bluff is more effective if the indications are that you are not on a draw. For example, at hold'em, it is better if there is no two-flush on the board.

(13) A check-raise on the end is almost never a bluff. If the player wanted to run a bluff, he would simply have led at the pot.

(14) A bluff that has outs can win the pot in two ways. They may fold, or you may hit a draw.

(15) An early bluff has the leverage of making the opponent consider how much it will cost him to play out the hand.

(16) You should consider a bluff any time the field has all checked on the previous round.

(17) With your starting hand, if you are going to overstate your values with a raise, be sure the hand is at least worth a call.

(18) If you know your opponent has a decent hand, it is seldom right at limit poker to try and make him lay it down.

(19) Do not try and help make your bluff work with a comment or gesture. If your bluff needs a touch of extra assistance to work, it likely should not have been made in the first place. Comments and gestures often have the reverse effect to what you desire.

(20) Poker is played for enjoyment as well as to win money. It is enjoyable to earn through a thoughtful play what you could not win by being lucky enough to have a superior hand. So have fun!

BLUFFING EXAMPLES

These are twelve hands where a successful steal of the pot was made by me. The hands were played at middle-size stakes in a limit hold'em game at Hollywood Park Casino in 1995. Each hand is followed by commentary explaining some facets of the play.

The cut-off seat is the name I like to use for the first seat to the right of the button, because a raise in that seat is an attempt to cut the button off from his privileged place of last to act. If he folds, you get his position.

HAND #1 $10-20   A♦-2♦   Little Blind

The pot is four-handed and unraised. The flop is 6♠-5♦-4♠. I check, the big blind bets, the other two players call, and I make a dubious call. My call is based on the fact that the betting is now closed for this round, I can pick up a nut diamond draw, and may possibly win the pot if I catch an ace or a three. But frankly, if either an ace or three comes, I plan to check, and probably will fold if someone bets, as either of those two cards can easily make someone a better hand than mine. The fourth street card is the J♥, an innocuous card. I check, and so does the rest of the field. The 7♠ comes on the end, making four cards to a possible straight on board. I bet. The big blind thinks for a few seconds and folds, and the others fold with no problem. My bluff wins.

COMMENTARY
(1) The field checked on the previous round.
(2) I am representing a specific hand, in this case a straight.
(3) I could easily have the hand I am representing. Hands in the blind may well consist of little cards, and should often represent such a holding in steal situations.
(4) The person who showed strength on an earlier round has players behind him to worry about. He would be much more likely to defend against a steal if he is the last person guarding the goal line.

104

BLUFFING EXAMPLES

HAND #2 **$10-20** **A♠-9♠** **Big Blind**

A player limps in up front, and only the little blind calls. I resist the strong impulse to raise, and rap the table. The flop is J♠-6♦-3♣. The little blind checks, and I bet trying to steal (although it is possible that I actually hold the best hand with ace-high). To my surprise, both opponents call. On fourth street comes the J♥. The little blind checks, I bet again, and both players fold.

COMMENTARY

(1) When a player checks and then calls after the flop, or is bet into and then calls, you do not know whether he is weak, or has a good hand and is slowplaying it until the limit goes up. But there are many more weak hands than good ones, so you are entitled to presume weakness until you get contrary evidence.

(2) I have an opinion on what both opponents hold—and what they do not hold. The player on my right likely has made a small pair from the flop-cards, and was hoping to improve. The player on my left could have a number of hands, including two overcards or a pocket pair. But I do not put him on a jack, because he is supposed to have a decent-size kicker with a jack for calling in early position before the flop. Top pair with a pretty good kicker would normally raise on the flop, since it is a holding where you think your hand is good, but would be content if the other players folded, since you are not that far out in front to make a drawout improbable.

(3) If I have what I am representing, which is top pair that just made trips, I am so far out in front that I am either uncatchable, or have them down to a two-outer (if they have a pocket pair). This factor is quite helpful in making a successful fourth street bluff.

HAND #3 **$10-20** **Q♣-J♣** **First**

BLUFFING EXAMPLES

The game so far has been passive with loose play, so I call the blind. A player in middle position calls, and the next player raises. The two players in the blind call the raise. I reraise, a form of semi-bluff that I might make only a couple of times a year. The whole field comes, so five of us stay to see the flop. The flop is 6♠-3♠-2♠, a low three-flush. All of us check. On fourth street comes the A♦. We all check again. I purposefully give a slight flinch, as if considering a bet. On the end comes the 2♣, pairing the board. The first two players check. I bet, and the field folds. My bluff wins.

COMMENTARY
(1) The reason I did not get called is that nobody had anything. It is possible that I was given credit for a hand such as A-K, which I suppose is plausible. But even if you are not given credit for much, most people who have nothing will simply fold, instead of putting a play on you.

(2) Once again, a pot was stolen on the end when everybody checked throughout. Note that the thief was getting 15-1 odds on his bet. At that kind of price, who can be honest?

HAND #4 $20-40   4♠-2♠   Cut-off Seat

I have changed seats and am required to post the big blind. I pick up my typical holding in this situation; four-high. Everybody folds around to me. I raise, and everyone throws their hand away.

COMMENTARY
(1) For some reason, a person who has a blind in the pot here is often given more credit for having something reasonable for his raise than a person who did not have any money in the pot. The truth is far different.

(2) Raising in this situation is such an attractive play that one should do so with any excuse. You are risking 1 bet to win 2.5 bets, as your bet that is already out there is now part of the pot. In the normal situation when you are not making up a blind, and so do not have any money in the pot, you would be risking

2 bets to win 1.5 bets. I would not criticize a player in this situation with a made-up blind and nobody yet in who raised the pot first, and then looked at his hand to see what he had.

HAND #5 $20-40   Q♥-J♥   Small Blind

Two players call before the flop. I raise (a play that I would not usually make). The big blind and other two players call, so four of us stay for the flop. The flop is a pretty good one for me; 10♠-9♥-4♠, giving me an open-ended straight-draw, a back-door flush-draw, and two overcards. I bet, the next two players fold, and the last player raises. I call.

On fourth street comes the 9♦. I check, he bets, and I call. The last card is the 6♦. I check, he bets, and I raise. He folds quickly; evidently he was on a draw and missed.

COMMENTARY
(1) The flop had a lot of drawing combinations, yet there was only one other player in the pot. When this player bets in an aggressive manner, there is a reasonable chance of his being on a draw, rather than having a made hand. It is often worthwhile investing a double bet trying to take the pot away from him on the end, either by check-raising, or raising him if he was acting first.
(2) You must not shrink from using a double bet as a bluff just because you are investing twice as much money as usual. Here I invested $80 to win $320, so I was still getting 4 to 1 on my money. My opponent was surely not a 4-1 underdog to be on a draw.
(3) One other advantage of this kind of bluff is they virtually never resteal the pot on a counter-bluff.

HAND #6 $6-12   6♣-6♠   MIDDLE POSITION

I open in middle position with a call of the blind. A player in late position raises and just the two of us take the flop. The flop

BLUFFING EXAMPLES

comes K♣-7♣-7♦, making a two-flush on the board. I check, he bets, and I raise, hoping to steal the pot. He reraises. I reluctantly call. Fourth street is the 8♥. I check, mentally prepared to give it up if my opponent bets. He checks. The last card is the K♠, counterfeiting any semblance of a hand that I may have had. I am reduced to playing the board. I bet, and my opponent folds. How sweet it is.

COMMENTARY

(1) My check-raise on the flop in a heads-up situation has a lot going for it. The only normal raising hands that could like this flop are A-A, K-K, and A-K. His reraise is a little suspicious, as most players with one of those hands listed above would likely just call on the flop, and come to the fore on the next betting round.

(2) My bet on the end seems automatic once my opponent dogs it on fourth street. The only strong hand he could conceivably hold to bet this way is pocket eights, which is really remote.

(3) A bluff always comes under consideration when it is a virtual certainty that you cannot win a showdown.

HAND #7 $20-40   K♥-J♠   SMALL BLIND

The player on my right was due for the big blind but left the game, so I had to post the big blind in the little blind position (two big blinds on this deal). A lady prop opened with a raise and I and the other big blind called, so three of us saw the flop. The board came A♣-A♦-6♠. I checked in first position, the player on my left checked, and the preflop raiser bet. I called, and the big blind folded. The fourth street card was the innocuous 3♠. I bet, and she folded.

COMMENTARY

(1) I (and others) often use the ploy of simply calling on the flop, to impress the opponent with the idea that I have a piece of the board. Then I bet on fourth street as a bluff.

(2) Note that a check-raise on the flop has the drawback of having a player behind me to worry about, as well as the raiser. It is a good idea to not commit a lot of your money until you see how the pot is going to develop. Also, my bet on fourth street is believable, because it looks like I could have just called on the flop with an ace in order to suck another player into the pot.

HAND #8 $15-30   8♥-7♥   BIG BLIND

A new player has posted a blind in the cut-off seat. A player calls up front, the new player raps, and the button and little blind call. I raise. The new player folds and the others call my raise, so four of us take the flop. The flop is Q♥-10♣-9♠. We all check. Fourth street is the K♦, making four cards to a straight on board, and again everybody checks. The last card is the A♥. I bet, and they all fold. Maybe I had checked a straight on fourth street, and maybe I decided to bet aces up when nobody could bet on the previous round.

COMMENTARY
(1) I think the situation that I had preflop is a good one for a funky play. My opponents showed appalling weakness by not raising when there was an extra blind posted on the deal. There was a chance that someone would fold, and they did. My hand is probably of close to average strength when compared to the others against me.
(2) Once again, I bet when there had been a lot of checking on previous rounds. It happens quite often that you are the preflop raiser, but are mentally done with it as soon as the ugly flop comes down. This typically happens where there are three callers (With only two, you probably would have bluffed a bet on the flop). But you should be prepared to make the proper mental adjustment when everybody checks. It is your responsibility as the preflop raiser to ensure that the money does not lie out there and rot. Think of yourself as doing those other players who are out a favor by trying to get the deal over

BLUFFING EXAMPLES

with as fast as possible. Be of public service. On this particular deal, I thought the fourth street card was too menacing for me to launch a bluff. But when they all checked a second time...

HAND #9 $9-18   J♥-9♥   BIG BLIND

A player who has been raising a lot of pots opens in early position with yet another raise, and gets two callers. I raise, and everyone calls. The flop is 10♠-6♠-5♣. I check, and the field checks behind me. On fourth street comes the 6♣. I bet, and the original raiser calls; the rest fold. Fifth street is a blank, the 2♥. I bet again, and this time the fellow folds.

COMMENTARY
(1) Once again, I have thrown in an extra raise on a hand that I was going to play anyway. Do not get the idea that I do this frequently; it is a rarity. But I would rather do this than raise on a hand that should be folded. If it were a cold two bets to me, I would not even consider making it three bets; I would simply fold.
(2) Here is another example where I dogged it on the flop, but turned aggressive again when the field checked.
(3) The bet again on the end seems automatic. There is a fairly large pot, my opponent has shown weakness, and I cannot win if I check.

HAND #10 $15-30   A♦-Q♦   BUTTON

The cut-off seat has posted a big blind because the blind had been missed in the regular order. A lady in early position who has been raising a lot of pots opens with yet another raise. The cut-off seat calls. I reraise, as it looks like I can make this play without giving up much, and may even hold the best hand, and they both call. The flop is K♠-8♣-3♦. They check, and I bet. The flop is not to my liking (I would prefer having two overcards if I am going to miss). Even so, there are only two opponents, so I must test them.

Unfortunately, they both call. On fourth street comes the K♥, pairing the board. They check again. This is such a good card to catch that I feel compelled to have another go at it. Particularly since the lady is an aggressive player, but has not made a move on this pot. I bet again, and they both cave in.

COMMENTARY

(1) My preflop reraise is reasonable, since I am going to call, and the person on my right is likely to be unhappy about putting in another bet. The other players are the enemy, so anything poker-wise that makes them unhappy usually pleases me. My reraise is likely to knock out the blinds and get some dead money into the pot.

(2) King-rag-rag is a good flop for representing a hand, as in raised or reraised pots the other players fear you have A-K. It is hard to see what the other players could have called me with on the flop. As there is no draw out there, somebody—everybody—is supposed to have a king. But sometimes, you cannot conceive of any hand they could have that makes sense, but you get the feeling that they are not so happy. Much of the time I would not bet again on fourth street with this type of flop. But here, everybody checked again, so I had another go at it. Had I been first, I would have checked on fourth street.

HAND #11 $10-20   9♥-4♣   BIG BLIND

The player in the cut-off seat enters the pot by limping in. The button and small blind call, so four of us see the flop in an unraised pot. The flop comes K♣-9♣-3♥, giving me second pair, no kicker. The flop is checked by all. Fourth street is the 3♣, pairing the board. If you are not going to bet here after the little blind checks, you should go over to the crap table, where your winning chances are evidently greater than in a poker game. I look at my holecards, look out at the board for a moment, and bet. All fold without a problem.

BLUFFING EXAMPLES

COMMENTARY

(1) It is likely from the betting that you hold the best hand. All checked the flop, and the 3♣ is not likely to help anyone.

(2) Despite the fact that I do not think of this bet as an actual bluff, I do not want to get called.

(3) When the board pairs small, the blind should be eager to represent trips, as he is the person who can represent holding a low card most credibly.

(4) I would be happy if the other players put me on trip threes instead of my actual hand of 9-4.

(5) The little trick of looking down at your holecards and then back out at the board looks for all the world like you are making sure your cards match the board. Naturally, you must use this type of ploy against strangers only, or the others will tumble to the fact that you do not have a hand when you do this. This look-back trick is especially effective for bluffing when there is four parts to a flush or straight on board. Have a friend do this trick while you watch, and you will see what a strong psychological play it is against a stranger. (For me, any of my regular opponents likely know that I do not ever need to look back again at my holecards during a deal to see what I have.)

HAND #12 $20-40   K♥-2♥   BIG BLIND

The cutoff seat has posted a blind, and raps the table in turn. The button raises. I call, and the cutoff calls, so three of us see the flop in a raised pot. The flop is A♠-J♠-4♠, making a three-flush on board. I check, the cutoff checks, and the button bets. I call, intending to bluff on fourth street. The cutoff folds, which is important, as I would not try a bluff if he had called. My call has had two good effects. It makes it look as if the flop was friendly, and it lets me know cheaply if the third player has anything. This play is used often when there is a pair or three-flush that came on the flop. Fourth street is the 2♠, making four spades on board. I bet, and the opponent folds rapidly.

COMMENTARY

(1) My background as a pot-limit player has made me very wary about making a big move on the pot while there are players other than my target that still have live hands. Sometimes an apparition appears out of the woodwork and unexpectedly throws a monkey wrench into your plans.

(2) There is no reason why the player who is the preflop raiser should have a piece of the board. Mathematically speaking, he is always an underdog to be helped by the flop.

(3) In this situation, it is hard to see how my opponent can call without a flush, and I am risking $60 to win $130, so my play is obviously sound poker.

A BLUFFING QUIZ

Knowing when to bluff is an important quality for a poker player. This skill is even more crucial at big-bet poker (pot-limit and no-limit play) than in limit games. I often find that the amount of money stolen by my bluffs is the difference between winning and losing during a poker session. To improve your quiz score, here are some guidelines that help a player decide when to fire chips for a hijacking.

It is desirable to have certain cards in your hand that reduce or prevent running into the nuts. A fairly frequent bluffing situation is the presence of a three-flush on board in a hold'em game when you have the lone ace of that suit. At hold'em, the ace of course also gives you a decent draw if there are cards to come. At Omaha, you can't make a flush with only one card of a suit in your hand, but having the "Ace of Trump" is still a key factor in venturing a bluff. Remember that at Omaha the other players are always afraid that the nuts is out against them.

For other board layouts, having key cards also improves your chance of running a successful bluff. Here are some examples:

(1) Having a card in your hand that matches the highest-ranking board-card seriously reduces the chance of running into top set.

(2) Having a pair in your hand of the rank needed to complete a straight on board considerably reduces the chances of someone having that straight. An example would be having a pair of kings in your hand with an A-Q-10 on the board.

(3) When launching a preflop steal, having an ace in your hand not only reduces the chance of running into the nuts (A-A), but also cuts down the possibility of being called by somebody with hands like A-K and A-Q.

It is nice when bluffing to have an out, a way of getting lucky and still winning the pot when your bet gets called. Outs are desirable, but not always essential. Some of the best bluffing situations arise when all the cards have been dealt. Often a bet is successful here because there are no outs, so the bettor cannot be betting on the come. He either has the holding represented, or he doesn't.

I am going to present you with four hands where you have the opportunity to make a play by a bet or raise. The quiz assumes that your table-image is normal; a person who sometimes bluffs, but not a habitual faker. It also assumes the opponent to be a reasonable player, and not the game's sheriff who dutifully prevents robberies.

Here are some big-bet poker situations where the question of whether to bluff arises. Look at each problem, decide on your answer, and see whether your feelings coincide with my opinion.

(1) No-limit hold'em—The flop is Q♥-J♥-7♣. You have K♣-10♣, an open-end straight-draw. The opponent bets and you call. The 3♣ comes on fourth street, giving you the added possibility of making a club flush. The opponent bets again, and you call. On the end comes the 2♥, making a possible flush on board— but not yours. The opponent checks, what do you do?

ANSWER—The opponent has placed you with a probable drawing hand. The most likely hand for you to hold is a flush-draw. You should "confirm his suspicions" by betting. He doesn't know your potential flush was in clubs, the backdoor suit. Chances are excellent that your opponent will fold. If it turns out that the fellow had been leading at the pot with the nut flush-draw in hearts, and checked when he made the flush, you have been outplayed, and are also very unlucky. The percentage play is to bluff. This situation comes up often, and is a good illustration why it is usually correct to just call on the flop with a straight-draw when there are two of a suit on the board. If the opponent has the flush working, your hand has been seriously weakened If he doesn't, maybe you will get the chance to pretend having it yourself. Also, playing a straight-draw

115

A BLUFFING QUIZ

fast on the flop with a two-flush on board invites your opponent to "err" by putting you on a flush-draw and calling or raising.

(2) No-limit hold'em—The flop is A♠-K♥-9♥. You hold A♥-7♥. You bet and get a caller. The 10♠ comes, and you decide to bet again. The caller again stays for your bet, and the J♦ comes on the end. The board now reads A♠-K♥-9♥-10♠-J♦ one card away from a straight. What should you do?

ANSWER—You should bet. Many players make the mistake of checking here because they have top pair. The fact is on this deal you are a heavy favorite to be beaten, and have invited a hijacking in the remote possibility that you have the superior hand. Many players make the mistake of failing to bluff when they have something, giving insufficient weight to whether their "something" is a realistic candidate to win the pot. In this example, your "something" has the chance of a knife against a gun, so you must feign a strong holding. It is very tough for the opponent to call without a straight at big-bet poker.

(3) Pot-limit Omaha—The flop is J♥-7♥-3♥, so there is a flush possibility. Your hand is A♥-J♦-J♣-9♣, giving you top set. Five people take the flop, and the player in the one-seat bets into the field. Everyone else folds, and it is up to you in last position. What is your play?

ANSWER—The player has undoubtedly flopped a flush. At pot-limit Omaha, there is nothing wrong with trying to make a player fold a flush You have the ace of hearts, and your opponent is almost surely aware of it. Do you have another heart with it or not? If he reads you for a "bluff," you have top set and the possibility of filling up and winning anyway. If you only flat-called on the flop with this hand instead of raising, please accept the Caspar Milquetoast award for cowardice. Maybe you should prefer video poker over big-bet poker. (These derogatory remarks do not apply if you flat-called with the intention of making a big play on **fourth street,** a very reasonable alternative idea.)

(4) Pot-limit Omaha—The flop is J♥-9♥-3♣. Your hand is A♥-K♥-7♦-6♦, giving you the nut flush-draw. Five people take the flop. The player in the one-hole bets, you call, and the rest of the field folds. On fourth street the J♠ appears, making an open pair of the highest-ranking card on board. The opponent checks; what is your action?

ANSWER—I would check. There is a high probability that my opponent bet a made hand on the flop, since my hand contains the two highest-ranking cards of the flush-draw. It is a commonplace play for a player who fills up when facing a probable drawing hand to check his filly. Even if the person drawing doesn't take the bait and bet, that player might hit his hand and pay off a bet on the end. Not only would I check my flush-draw here, but there is a good possibility that I would fold if I made the flush on the end and my opponent then bet.

These are a few of the ideas that should run through your head when contemplating a bluff. For those of you who have difficulty putting a lot of money into the pot without a good hand, you probably have the image of a rock and would be more effective for a while than the average player in bluffing successfully. Let your hair down and go for it.

SETTING HOLD'EM STANDARDS

Let us suppose that you set a specific standard for what hands you will enter a pot on when you are first to act in a typical nine-handed limit hold'em game. What factors would cause you to modify those standards for a particular game?

Before answering this question, let us examine those standards. Here are the guidelines that I used for the typical $15-$30 and $20-$40 limit hold'em games that I played in every day at Hollywood Park Casino when I was working there as a proposition player. (These are the standards that actually evolved after I had been working there for a while, as I was slightly looser than this at first.)

(1) Pairs—7-7 or better
(2) Suited cards—J-10 or better
(3) Unsuited cards—A-J, K-Q (I folded A-10, K-J, and Q-J)

What would cause me to loosen these starting requirements for a certain game? Naturally, if some players are away from the table, the game becoming shorthanded would relax my standards. But for the purpose of this article, let us assume that the game stays ninehanded. What would loosen my play, and how would it do so?

There is only one thing that would cause me to lower my standards. That would be if far fewer pots were being raised preflop in my game than in a normal game. In this type of tempo, there will be more players than usual contending the pot.

For passive games as described, how should your standards be affected? I think the smaller pairs now become playable. A set is still a set, and you want to try for one if you think you can do so cheaply. Perhaps you can play a couple more suited connectors such as 10-8 suited or 9-8 suited, though to me this seems more like just gambling rather than having an overlay.

There is one thing you must not do in a passive game with volume pots. Do not lower your standards for unsuited cards. In volume pots, big unsuited cards go down in value. So you still should throw away hands up front such as A-10, K-J, and Q-J, no matter how loose or how passive a game may be.

Let us now look at the other side of the coin; fast-paced games where pots are raised far more often than not. How should our standards be affected in that case?

I feel the best way of handling the situation described is to avoid playing hands in first position that you would not want to come in for a raised pot if you had to cold-call that raise. I feel you should fold pairs smaller than 9-9, and consider folding A-J offsuit and K-Q offsuit. Even with suited cards, you would need to tighten up. Hands such as A-x suited, 10-9 suited, J-9 suited, Q-10 suited, and Q-9 suited are good candidates for the muck.

I don't claim the standards and modifications given in this article are indisputably precise. They are simply what I use and believe in, and they have worked for me. You could alter them somewhat to suit your style. But most pros have something close to this that they go by, so you shouldn't make a radical departure.

In view of the preceding discussion, you can see where many players have a big leak in their play. They get into a game where the money flows liberally. Many pots are being raised preflop. Naturally, when the caliber of hands needed to raise the pot goes down, the caliber of hands needed to reraise the pot also goes down. A lot of pots are "three bets," and even "cap." Yet the hand values needed to play preflop, which should be tightened, are even loosened by a lot of people. Hands worth only one bet are getting backed for two, three, or four bets. The average player gets involved on far too many hands for this type of game. People seem to attach too much importance to the fact that the raisers really do not have hands good enough to be raising, and forgetting the nature of their own hand. When all you have is a pair of sixes, it does not make much difference if the raisers hold A-9 suited or K-J offsuit instead of real raising hands like A-K or A-Q.

Let's look at a typical hand that is misplayed in a fast game. A player is dealt 6-6 under the gun. He feels there is a good chance nobody can beat the hand at this point—and may well be right—so he calls the blind. If some players trail in behind him and nobody raises, he is getting involved from a sound foundation. His 6-6 may win unimproved, and he is only paying a small price for the chance to win a big pot by flopping a set.

But look how things change for a 6-6 when the pot is raised or reraised. The extra money in before the flop means that people are staying in after the flop with the hope of pairing their overcards. Those overcards will almost surely come on fourth or fifth street, if they do not hit on the flop. (If they don't come, that 6-6 may be in even worse shape, as people will be making trips or a straight with all those small cards on the board.) So the 6-6 will likely need to make a set to win in a raised pot. Yet those small pairs are paying too much money to do this, since the odds on flopping a set at hold'em are about 7.5 to 1 against doing so with a pocket pair. So any way you look at it, it is wrong to play a pair of sixes or the like if you expect that the pot will be raised behind you, even though there will be multihanded action.

People describe a game as "loose" if a lot of chips are being put into the pot. But "loose" is far too generic a word to go by when planning your preflop strategy. What you really need to know is the frequency with which the pots are being raised. In a loose game where lots of people play before the flop but seldom raise, you can lower your starting requirements. But if it is a loose game where a lot of pots are getting popped, you must tighten your starting requirements.

SOME HOLD'EM HANDS

I thought it could be helpful for you if I chronicled the hands I played in a one-hour time period in the $20-$40 limit hold'em game at the Hollywood Park cardroom. I think that might be more educational in some ways than simply giving generalities. Naturally, I cannot claim every action I took was "the correct play," but I always had a reason for my actions. So here goes.

Hand #1 — I pick up A♦-J♦ in first position to the left of the button. The game has just started, so I am going to play the hand in an aggressive manner. Nearly all the players in the game are strangers to me, so I want to look like a person willing to give some action. I open for a raise, and get called only by the blinds. The flop comes down K♥-6♠-4♥, which of course does nothing for me. The opponents both check. I bet, because the flop may not have helped them, and they should be given an opportunity to throw their hands away. Alas, the big blind calls me, although he seems a bit hesitant. Since the caller is a total stranger, it is hard for me to tell if the hesitation is real or feigned. On fourth street comes the 10♣, giving me the possibility of a gutshot queen for a straight. He checks again. I bet. Since the limit doubles on fourth street, it is hard to hold back from betting when you're heads-up against an opponent who may be quite weak. He calls me without a problem. The last card is an unhelpful 10♦, pairing the board. My opponent checks. His "body English" says he's not too happy. Even so, I simply check along with him. I do have an ace-high to show down, and if he can beat it, he is going to call me. He shows a Q-J offsuit, so I win the pot with my ace. He called me on the flop with absolutely nothing, and picked up a straight-draw on fourth street to continue contending. I mentally mark him as a very loose calling-type player.

Hand #2 — I pick up Q♣-9♣ in the small blind. The pot is not raised, so I put in ten more dollars to call. There are four of us in

SOME HOLD'EM HANDS

for the flop. It comes Q♠-8♠-3♠, giving me top pair. I bet and the button calls. Fourth street is the A♣. An ace is never a happy card to see unless it helps you, as it could easily help an opponent. However, it would be pusillanimous to check in a heads-up situation when holding a real hand. I bet, and my opponent pops me with a raise. If my opponent is not bluffing, I am down to no more than five outs, and may well have none. Therefore, my fold is quick and easy.

Hand #3 — I pick up two kings in middle position. Naturally, I open with a raise. Only the big blind calls. It is the loose player who was my opponent on hand #1. The flop comes 8-8-3 of three different suits. This is not that good of a flop for me despite the raggedy appearance. I would prefer to see something like J-6-3 or 10-5-3, where I can make some money after the flop and still have the best hand. To my surprise, the opponent leads into me. I think most players would raise here, but I don't care to do this. If he has something I can beat, I'd like to see him lead again on fourth street. If he doesn't have three eights, then he has very few outs. The fourth street card is a real ugly one; another three. My opponent hesitates, then bets. The hesitation is noticeably different in character than the hesitation he had on that previous deal when he didn't have anything. It looks to me like he may have just put a bad drawout on me. Nevertheless, I am not going to throw away my two kings at limit poker. I call his bet, and then call him again at the river when a blank comes. My opponent tables a K-3 offsuit. Naturally, this grates on me a bit, as I reflect on what the price had been before the flop on this player beating my two kings with his one lonely three.

Hand #4 — I pick up 9-9 in the big blind. Two people limp in, the loose goose and a lady on his left. The flop comes an unhelpful A-K-6. Normally after raising the pot I would take one stab at winning it by betting this type of flop. Here, I refrain from doing so. The loose goose will call me on any gutshot, and perhaps an even worse holding. What will I do on fourth street if I bet now and get called? So I check. The loose goose also checks, and the lady bets. I fold, and L.G. calls. The hand is checked out the rest of the way. They both show down a king, and the lady wins the pot with a bigger sidecard.

I realize these hands are not thrilling; they weren't meant to be. But they do illustrate some typical situations that arise at limit hold'em. And if you look closely, some lessons can be drawn.

(1) Not every pro would handle these hands precisely as I did; perhaps few would. there is room for individual style, and it is easy to make an error.

(2) A lot of attention was paid as to who was in the pot. The presence of a loose calling type of player can easily change your normal strategy.

(3) When you are heads-up with a reasonable hand that was good enough to bet the flop, it is seldom right to check on fourth street just because an unpleasant card comes. With only one opponent, he is an underdog to have been helped.

(4) A hand with ace-high that never helps should check after all the cards are out. The opponent is very likely to call a bet if he can beat you, and very likely to fold if he cannot. Save your bluffs for hands that have virtually no chance otherwise.

(5) Heads-up at limit poker a big pair is a through ticket.

A TYPICAL HAND

Here is a hand I played in the $20-$40 limit hold'em game at Hollywood Park Casino when I was working there as a proposition player. Even though it is a routine hand, it does illustrate a few points that I would like to make.

I picked up K♣-2♣ in the little blind. Everyone folded around to me. It is my personal policy not to "chop." Most hold'em players in Southern California chop the pot when in the blind and all the other players have folded. This means the big and little blind each take back the blinds they have posted, instead of playing out the pot. This arrangement is allowed by the house and is not considered tacky at all. Since chopping gets a deal over with immediately, I certainly have nothing to complain about if others in the game want to chop.

I don't like to chop myself for several reasons. The main one is I am a conservative player when it comes to entering pots, so I don't get to play much. Dueling when in the blind helps me relieve the boredom of sitting out, thus making it easier to keep discipline waiting for a good hand in other poker situations. Another reason is there are a number of people who are weaker players, and one hopes to make some money from them in the long run by playing out the pots. Rather than trying to single out such players and selectively refusing to chop, it is easier for me to just play out the pots with everybody, including my good friends. They understand the situation.

Anyway, I just call with my suited K-2. Yes, my hand is a slightly above average one for heads-up play, but this does not mean I should raise the pot. I am out-of-position, which means I really don't have that much going for me. One thing I want to know early is whether my opponent is the sort of player who habitually raises in the big blind if the little blind limps in. Besides, if he sees that I sometimes limp in, perhaps he will get out of my way and let me pick up the blind money with a raise at some future moment when I am feeling more ambitious. On this occasion the big blind rapped the table, declining to raise.

The flop came to my liking: K♥-Q♠-8♠, giving me top pair. There are a lot of drawing possibilities, and fourth street could clutter the board even more, so I simply bet my hand. Betting the flop gives you information about the opponent's hand, among its other benefits. This makes it easier to play good poker later on. I seldom check the flop when a good spread comes for me. (The main exception would be when there is a good reason to expect the other person to bet.) I want **someone** to bet the flop, so I do it myself.

On this occasion, my opponent raised me. This type of raise could be made for a number of reasons:

(1) My opponent thinks he has a good hand.

(2) My opponent wants to find out if I really have something.

(3) My opponent is drawing. In this case, he may be planning to check on fourth street if he does not complete his hand, having "saved" a half-bet by raising at the lower limit to get a free card at the higher limit.

When only two of us stay for the flop, hand values change considerably. Top pair is a pretty fair holding. There is no way I would consider folding top pair at this early stage, despite my weak kicker. Should I reraise him? My hand does not look so good to me that it will be played to the end no matter what comes. For example, the 10♠ would be an ugly enough fourth street card for me to abandon ship if my opponent bet again. So I simply call the raise.

On fourth street comes a sweetheart; the 2♦, giving me two pair. I bet right out, for two reasons. First, there is too great a danger that if I check, the opponent will simply take a free card. His raise on the flop is by no means a commitment to bet on fourth street. Second, a bet by me will not reveal the fact that the deuce gave me two pair. My opponent is going to assume that I am betting because none of the possible draws got there. He'll know that I probably have a made hand, but he's unlikely to make any sort of big laydown.

A TYPICAL HAND

My opponent calls the fourth street bet. On the end comes the 6♠, making a three-flush on the board. This of course is not a pleasing sight. Nevertheless, I bet again. When your opponent has the big blind in an unraised pot, it is far less likely that he is suited than if he had entered the pot voluntarily after looking at his hand. I see people misguidedly dogging decent hands on the end all the time, panic-stricken because of a possible flush. The question should not be if there is any possibility of a flush, but whether the opponent is likely to have it.

In this case my opponent gave me a crying call. When I showed him my two pair, he flashed me a king and discarded his hand.

Hands like this one are typical for limit hold'em these days. Because the bet on the flop is really only a half-bet, a lot of opponents raise on hands far short of rock-crusher status. In fact, many players will delay raising until the limit doubles if they have a high-caliber holding. It is important that you not get run over when you are out-of-position. Don't be afraid to call a raise on the flop when holding a decent hand. And don't be afraid to bet if fourth street is a blank or helps you. Your opponent's raise on the flop does not oblige him to bet fourth street if you check. At poker, as in life, if you want to make sure something will be done, do it yourself.

HOW MANY ENEMY?

One mistake I frequently see is someone to show a blatant disregard for the number of players that stayed for the flop. In later betting, it is a clear error to try and bully a large field. Unfortunately, quite a few players pay scant attention to how many opponents they have. They think the raiser is supposed to bet the flop whenever the other people check, as if the number of opponents is meaningless. This is foolishness.

Once in a while I play in a lowstakes game, where the number of players in each pot is usually quite a bit higher than at the more expensive tables. Even so, there is often a player in the game who is willing to take on a whole crowd with a weak hand in a determined effort to purchase the pot. I cannot help thinking he has a bit of General George Custer in him; brave to a fault, and not seeming to care how many Indians are arrayed against him. Figuratively speaking, he usually suffers a similar fate.

I once saw a guy in this kind of game raise the pot on the button with a pair of eights (a pretty aggressive play in itself). About six other players stayed for the flop, which came A-J-3 with a two-flush. When everybody checked, he bet right out. His chance of having the best hand was virtually nil, as was his chance that everyone would fold, or that he would help his hand by catching an offsuit eight. He got called by three players, and then unsuccessfully fired another barrel on fourth street. It was close to Christmas, so perhaps he was feeling philanthropic.

Here is another example. You raise the pot preflop on A-K and get called. The flop comes ragged; we'll use J-5-2 offsuit as an example. Against one or two opponents, it is clear to bet the flop. You might have the best hand, and perhaps can win the pot right there. If you get called, your bet on the flop may have at least gained you a free card on fourth street. Alternatively, you may wish to fire again and have another go at it. It takes a complete wimp to dog A-K by checking a flop like that in a shorthanded pot.

HOW MANY ENEMY?

But suppose the whole field comes for your preflop raise. If you are on the button and eight players check it to you (on that same ragged flop), will you bet? I certainly wouldn't. The extra pot odds by the added preflop money from all those players means you are surely going to get called. In fact, I'd say you are better than even money to get check-raised. When nine people stay for the flop, someone almost always turns a good hand. Prudence dictates checking it back on the flop.

When I was a child, my aunt read to me Tennyson's famous poem, "Charge of the Light Brigade." I could not understand how those men could sally forward into almost certain death. Perhaps their spirit has been caught by a number of brave but foolish poker players. They keep charging the pot, no matter how many guns are arrayed against them. If poker represents a form of warfare, remember that a general must consider the probable enemy strength before committing his troops to battle. Perhaps you should think of playing poker as a military campaign, where you have a goal that you want to reach, and knowing the number of enemy soldiers is a critical piece of information needed for the right campaign decisions.

To see the change in strategy that takes place at poker as the number of enemy soldiers rises, we should contrast the extremes. We will analyze what takes place with only one opponent, and then analyze what happens in a "family pot" where all are in.

With only one opponent, the key word is aggression. Your opponent does not rate to hold a good hand, and if you can get him to fold, you win the pot. Most of the time, you bet. Once in a while, you check-raise, and once in a while you check and fold.

Note that here the nature of your hand is not as critical to how you play. With a weak hand, you bet and try to steal the pot. With a mediocre hand, you bet to see if the opponent has anything. If you are lucky enough to pick up a good hand, you bet because you want to either make some money or induce surrender. Notice how checking fails to help you accomplish your goals. The main reasons you check every once in a while in heads-up situations is to avoid being too predictable, or because the early betting has marked your opponent with a good hand.

With the whole field still in after the first betting round, the nature of your hand is extremely important. It is practically impossible to win the pot by a bet or raise. The pot-winner is going to have to show the best hand after all the cards are out. Poker skills such as aggressiveness, willingness to bluff, and the ability to pick up tells are next to worthless. The primary poker skills needed are proper hand evaluation and knowledge of the odds on completing a particular draw. In a family pot, you are playing "showdown poker," because the best hand at the end will win.

The extremes of one opponent and a whole tableful of opponents make the appropriate strategy for those situations pretty obvious. But what about all the intermediate situations, which are much more common? I think a good way to look at the various possibilities is to take a particular poker hand and see how the play of it changes based on the number of opponents. We will assume the game is limit hold'em for all our examples.

Suppose you pick up the A♥-K♥, and are in the little blind. The pot is unraised when the betting reaches you, so you of course raise. The flop comes down J♣-8♣-3♦, which is not of much help to your hand. You are first; do you check or bet? Let us examine your decision with differing numbers of enemy soldiers against you.

Against one opponent, you bet. The odds actually favor your having the best hand. He is not likely to have started with a pocket pair, and it is about two to one the flop did not make him a pair.

Against two opponents, I would also bet. I am only a bit less than even money to have the best hand, and I have outs (six of them) that could help me draw out if I am behind. Note that there are now six half-bets in the pot, and I am betting only one half-bet, so even if I am a favorite to get called, I am taking a mathematically sound action.

Against three opponents, we are getting much closer to the point where I should pull in my horns. With this particular flop, I would still probably bet more often than not. But it is a close decision, and not an automatic one at all. Make a slight change in the flop to make it more threatening, such as making that 8♥ the 9♥, and I would favor a check.

Against four or more opponents, I would definitely check. Someone figures to have made a good hand. I am very likely to get called. There is also the greatly increased possibility that my "six outs" will not get me out, but instead cost me quite a bit of extra money. Someone may have two pair or better, make such a hand with an ace or king that I need, or simply get lucky and buy help along the way somewhere. With four or more opponents, you need a real hand to bet. Heck, it is risky enough to bet when you actually **hold** a big pair here, so why try to represent one?

Let us look at another situation at hold'em. Suppose you are on the button with the A♠-9♠ in an unraised pot. The flop comes K♥-9♣-5♦, giving you second pair. Everyone checks to you; what is your action?

To answer this question intelligently, we need more information. How many Indians are out there? Let us see how our action changes with the number of opponents.

(1) With one opponent you bet without any problem.
(2) With two opponents, it is still pretty automatic to bet.
(3) With three opponents, you now have some kind of decision to make. My inclination would still be to bet, but I would be influenced to some degree by whether the opponents were the kind that frequently check their good hands.
(4) With four or more opponents, I would almost surely check. I do not believe in betting borderline hands into a crowd, even if they have all checked.

As you can see from these examples, I treat the presence of two opponents in the majority of cases as not being enough to inhibit me from playing aggressive poker. The presence of four or more opponents I treat with the same philosophy as a family pot, in that I do not bet unless I think that I have the best hand. For me, the most difficult number of opponents for judging the right action is three. It is much more difficult to run three opponents out of the pot than only two, but it can still be done.

For those difficult fourhanded pots, where there are three opponents, you need to be sensitive to the number of card combinations that are created with each flop, paying particular attention to the number of higher-ranking cards, which in a sane game are more likely to fit the cards held by the opposition. Lacking a real hand, I do not try too hard for the pot when the majority of the flop cards are in the high zone. For example, a flop of Q-7-5 is not nearly as dangerous as a flop of Q-10-5. Naturally, the presence of a two-flush increases the chance that the flop helped someone. Also, your opponents are more likely to call on a marginal hand, hoping you are drawing.

So if you want to improve your poker, it is necessary to become a good general. Gauge the enemy strength before deciding on your course of action. There is no medal of honor awarded at poker for extraordinary bravery. When you take on a large group of warriors with an inferior weapon, expect to get scalped!

RAISING AND MISSING

It is a pleasant feeling to survey your holecards on a new deal and see hands such as A-K or A-Q. If I have one of these hands and nobody else has raised the pot, I am very likely to make it two bets. But when the flop comes down and I have neither a pair nor a flush-draw, the pleasant feeling abruptly leaves. Now I have to play poker and see if anything can be salvaged on the deal.

Since it is about 2-1 against helping big slick (A-K) and similar hands by making a pair or better, getting stranded after the flop with a fair amount of money in the pot and very little hand left is an all-too-familiar hold'em occurrence. And how you do in the game depends in no small measure how you handle this type of situation.

Some people handle this scenario very badly. They simply pretend every time that they have a big pair in the pocket and fire chips like a maniac. Others get so disgusted with missing flops that they stop raising pots on big cards, and wait for the big pairs. I don't catch enough big pairs to restrict my raising to those hands. When you see the kind of trash many people see flops with, it is simply common sense to charge them a double bet when you have a decent hand. So we need to talk about when to bet when you raise and miss.

It is important to realize that your unimproved hand has depreciated immensely in value. If more than one opponent is still in the pot, you do not figure to have the best hand. Nor do you have a good draw. Only six cards help you pair, and 41 do not, which leaves you about a 6 to 1 underdog to buy a pair on the next card. Sometimes making a pair is not enough to win. Somebody can have you drawing dead, and there is a possibility a card that pairs you makes another player two pair. So make that mental adjustment and realize that what used to be a fine hand before the flop has been reduced to a third-rate holding.

The most important element in deciding whether to check or bet after the flop is the number of opponents that stayed for the flop. If you are heads-up, there is a better-than-even chance against most people that your unimproved A-K is still the best hand. So with only one opponent betting is pretty automatic.

On the other end of the spectrum, it is foolish to fire into a large crowd. My rule-of-thumb is to not bother betting into four or more opponents. Someone is going to have a better hand than you, and they are unlikely to get pried loose from it. Even the strategy of taking one stab at the pot in order to get a free card on fourth street may well backfire, as most players (often incorrectly) check a good hand on the flop expecting the raiser to bet. There is a good chance of getting check-raised when a whole crowd knuckles it to you. So I don't feel there is any kind of real decision to be made about whether to bet unless you are up against specifically two or three opponents.

Let's talk about what to do when you raise and miss in a three-handed or four-handed deal. The general guidelines are whether you still have a hand that has some value, whether the flop looks like it is likely to have helped the opponents, and whether there is something you can represent. Here are some flops. Pretend you have three opponents, have raised on A♠-Q♠, and are first to act. Should you bet?

(1) 10♥-9♥-7♦   Check. With three parts to a straight on the board your opponents are likely to have something good. Two overcards may well be drawing dead.

(2) 9♣-6♦-2♥   Bet. This is obvious when the flop is small and raggedy.

(3) J♣-9♥-3♦   Check. With two flop-cards (J and 9) in the intermediate zone, you are very likely to get played with. The two-flush on board is also a drawback.

(4) K♥-7♦-3♣   Bet. The opponents may be afraid you have A-K and fold.

RAISING AND MISSING

(5) J♠-10♥-3♣ I would bet because a king on fourth street gives me the nut straight. I also have a backdoor spade draw, which is not a lot, but still a consideration. Be more aggressive when you have some extra outs.

(6) K♦-9♥-8♥ Check. Sure, there is a king on the board, but those two touching suited cards with it make it most unlikely your opponents will all surrender.

(7) J♣-6♥-3♦ Bet. With only one big card on board have a go at it.

(8) K♣-9♥-6♦ Check. There are so many possible straight-draws you will surely get played with. There is no easy way to know if you are up against a gutshot draw or a good hand, and any fourth street card above a four could help the enemy.

Of course, these layouts don't come close to covering all the bases. They are just to get you thinking along the right track. Some other factors in your decision whether to check or bet are your position, your present table image, and who is in the pot with you. Even so, I feel the two most important influences on what to do when you raise with two big cards and come up empty are the number of opponents and the texture of the flop. Making the right decision after you raise and miss at limit hold'em will have a major effect on your poker bankroll.

PLAYING THE BLIND POSITION

One of the most difficult decisions for a limit hold'em player is how to play when in the blind. I believe it is easier to judge which hands to play when you don't have any money in the pot yet then to know what to play when you are partway in.

Being in the blind can be a trap for the weaker players. Like a shopper that can't resist a bargain, they play a lot of hands because they are getting a reduced price. Yet the problems stemming from getting involved with a weak hand out-of-position are considerable.

I do not view the strategy that most players use in the blind as being correct. In fact, my attitude is the exact opposite of what might be termed the conventional wisdom. Let me explain through the use of a brief quiz.

Suppose you hold a good drawing hand such as a J-10 suited, and are in the small blind. Would you rather see one player call the blind or three players call the blind?

Nearly all poker players would give an answer something like this: "I would rather see three players call and play a five-way pot. I have a good drawing hand, and with drawing hands you want multihanded action." Of course, I agree with this answer.

Now let me pose a somewhat similar problem, but one I feel is fundamentally different. Suppose you pick up a J-7 offsuit in the small blind. Once again, the problem is whether you would prefer one caller or three callers to the blind bet. What do you say?

I think most players would instantly reply "Three callers," and use the same logic as in the previous problem to explain their choice. But I have a strong preference for only one caller (making a threehanded pot). Let me explain.

There is a big difference between a J-10 suited and a J-7 offsuit. The J-10 suited is an excellent drawing hand, whereas that J-7 offsuit is simply a piece of garbage. The J-10 suited has a decent chance to make a good hand and win on the merits; a J-7 offsuit does not.

PLAYING THE BLIND POSITION

There are two basic ways of winning a pot. The first way is to show the best hand at the end; the second way is to make an uncalled bet. So every poker hand actually may be said to have two values. The hand has intrinsic value in terms of the likelihood of it being the best hand at the end. But it also has "stealing value," because as long as it is a live hand, the owner has the possibility of making a winning bet or raise.

Let us return to our dog of J-7 offsuit. Even though any two cards can turn to gold with the right boardcards, the intrinsic value of this hound is quite small. Yet simply being a paid member of the pot means the hand has "stealing value."

If you were hoping to steal a pot by a bet, would you rather try and steal from two other players or four other players? We all know that it is much easier to steal from only two. In fact, even knowing there is twice as much strange money in the pot would not persuade you to go up against four opposing players in a hijack effort.

I think it is a mistake to wish for a large number of players when you have a bad hand. I would rather have fewer players and a better chance to steal the pot. A good drawing hand and a dog are different hands and demand different treatment.

Put into concrete terms, holding a J-7 in the little blind, I would call (in a betting structure where I was halfway in) only if there was a threeway pot. With more than two other players, I am panic-stricken that the only way for me to win the pot will be to show down the best hand, which is quite unlikely.

Many players seem to have the idea that it is okay to play a dog if you are getting sufficient odds. In one respect I agree. For example, suppose a player has the big blind in a no-limit hold'em tournament with a structure of $100 ante and blinds of $200 and $400. A player opens for $800 all-in, the rest of the other players fold, and the action comes back to the big blind. In a nine-handed game the big blind is getting odds of 23 to 4 on his money; nearly 6 to 1. At a price like that, it is highly questionable whether he should look at his hand before calling the raise. Against only one opponent, getting good odds justifies a call.

PLAYING THE BLIND POSITION

But the situation encountered at a money limit hold'em game is not like that at all. Even though the pot odds may be quite favorable, you have a large field of opponents to beat, instead of just one player. And you can't shoot a bunch and steal the pot; you're restricted to a peashooter. That means your dog has got to stand up against an array of better hands.

So the next time you pick up a puppy, don't get mesmerized by big pot odds if there is a whole crowd to beat. Rather, think about how difficult it is to defeat an army without a good weapon. It is hard enough to make J-J stand up against a big field, let alone a J-7. Any two will **not** do if the number of contestants is so large there will be a showdown.

A HOLD'EM QUIZ

Here are a dozen problems whose setting is a mid-sized limit hold'em game; say $20-40 (Blinds of $10 and $20). I give my preferred answer at the end of each question for convenience, but be a sport and cover my answer until you have chosen your own. On each problem, there may be anywhere from zero to all answers considered right, so give all the selections you think apply. These questions are designed to illustrate a lot of the pointers that I give my students. These of course are my own answers, which in a few cases may run counter to the ideas of others.

(1) You are on the button and nobody has yet opened. What is the order of preference for hands to open with a raise?

(A) Q♥-10♥   **(B)** A♠-9♣   **(C)** 9♦-8♦

Answer – 1st (B) A♠-9♣   2nd (A) Q♥-10♥   3rd (C) 9♦-8♦
When going for a steal, being suited is less important than having high cards. Having a hand with an ace in it is helpful, as you have something you can show down that figures to beat a busted draw. I would definitely raise on both the ace-nine offsuit and queen-ten suited. The third hand, suited connectors, my inclination would be to fold unless I knew the big blind to be a tight player.

(2) The game is ten-handed and you are first to act. Which hands do you play?

(A) A♠-8♠   **(B)** 5♥-5♦   **(C)** K♥-10♥

Answer – All of these hands should be folded up front in the typical $20-40 game in Nevada or California. The one thing they all have in common is you do not want to have to pay a double bet to see the flop. These hands can be played in passive lowstakes games, but not under the stated conditions for this problem.

138

(3) You are playing in a game where the play has been straight-forward. The pot is opened up front for a raise and the button makes it three bets. You are in the big blind. Which of these hands would you use to cap it at four bets?

(A) A♥-K♥   **(B)** Q♦-Q♣   **(C)** K♥-K♣

Answer – I would only cap the pot with the kings. Sometimes it is a good idea to cap it with any hand you are going to play. But here, the extra bet does not figure to get anybody out. In terms of hand values, you need aces or kings to cap it when a solid player raises someone who opened under the gun.

(4) The pot is four-handed and unraised. You were in the big blind. The flop is K♣-9♣-6♥. Which of these hands would you call a bet on your right with?

(A) K♠-8♦   **(B)** J♥-10♥   **(C)** 10♦-9♦

Answer – None of the above. Top pair with a weak kicker in a four-handed pot is a dubious holding, and a bet coming through you by someone who leads off betting into a crowd means you are unlikely to have the best hand. Even if the bettor is on a draw, someone else may gave you beaten, or he may make his draw. Obviously, if you are not supposed to call with top pair, you should also fold second pair.

(5) The field of three other players in an unraised pot checks to you on the button. The texture of flop offering the best chance for a successful bluff is:

(A) Axx   **(B)** Kxx   **(C)** xxx

Answer – A lot of people will call you holding two overcards to the board, so I do not think the chance of a successful steal is that great when all rags flop. A hand with an ace in it figures to get played, and it is easier to check aces than any other pair, as there are no overcards to worry about if the field checks. I think the flop that offers the best prospect for a successful steal is hand (B), Kxx.

(6) At limit hold'em, position is most valuable with how many opponents?

(A) One   **(B)** Two or three   **(C)** Four or five

Answer – I think two or three is the ideal number of opponents when you have position. One opponent is not afraid to use a lot of deception in the play of the hand. With four or five opponents, you may be able to use your position to save a bet at some point, but you are most unlikely to use it to actually win the pot. With that many players, the best hand normally wins.

(7) You are in the big blind. The flop is K♠-10♣-5♠. A four-handed pot is bet by the first player; you are second. Which hands do you raise with?

(A) J♠-10♠   **(B)** A♠-9♠   **(C)** Q♣-J♣

Answer – With hand (A), a pair and a flush-draw that is not the nut draw, you would like to narrow the field, so a raise is advisable. With hand (B), the nut flush-draw, your hand is strong enough to raise, but you do not want to knock out any straight-draws or small flush-draws, so a simple call is the best action. With hand (C), a straight-draw, raising with a flush-draw on the board is poor poker, as your hand is too weak.

(8) You are in the blind with a 9-3 offsuit. Two players call, so you are first in a three-handed pot. The flop is all strangers: K♣-8♦-2♥. You check, and the others also check. Fourth street is the innocuous 4♣. What percentage of the time would you bet out and try for a steal of the pot?

(A) 25%-40%   **(B)** 55%-70%   **(C)** 85%-100%

Answer – If you only steal about a third of the time here, you are only winning your "fair share" of three-handed pots. We aspire to win more than our "fair share." In addition, you are the player who has the right of first bluff, and the only player who can reasonably represent that 4♣ as helping you. Answer (A) is too conservative to suit me. As for answer (C), it is not a good idea to be too predictable in your play. I like answer (B) the best.

(9) Which of these statements about betting on the end are accurate?

(A) A player who bluffs is usually busted, with no hope of winning a showdown.
(B) A check-raise on the end is almost never a bluff.
(C) Bluffing is usually done by a player while he is drawing rather than after he has missed, so most of the time you should not call holding only one pair when someone bets on the end.

Answer – (A) is true, as a player with even a small pair is not nearly as likely to bluff as one who has a hopeless hand. (B) is true, as a player with nothing who intends to bluff will normally bet out, not wanting to risk the possibility you might simply show down your hand and win if he checks. (C) is false. Stealing on the end is sufficiently common that you are often forced to call on the end with a weak hand, because the pot odds are so high you cannot afford to fold a hand that might win. Of course, it helps to know your players.

(10) Normally, the maximum number of players you should try to bluff from first position is:

(A) three   **(B)** four   **(C)** five

A HOLD'EM QUIZ

Answer – Bluffing into more than three opponents is dangerous and very seldom succeeds. My answer is (A).

(11). The winning style of play is:

(A) Tight to start, tight with a large number of opponents, and aggressive in heads-up and threeway pots.
(B) Very solid at all times.
(C) Highly aggressive. It is okay to contest a lot of pots if you are the one who is doing the betting.

Answer – (A) is the style of play favored by most top players. You can try to play in style (C) like our current World Champion Stu Ungar seems to, but you are not going to get his results. It takes one heck of a poker player to play this way and not simply be throwing a party. As for always playing super-solid, you may be a winning player, but you are not maximizing your potential unless you are aggressive in shorthanded pots.

(12) Which statements about bluffing are true and will help you be a winner?

(A) You must give a lot of action to get a lot of action.
(B) You have got to advertise, so budget some money for it.
(C) Don't bluff unless you think it is the right play.

Answer – The only statement I agree with is (C). My advertising budget is zero. Of course, I sometimes bluff, but not to try and create a wild image or to get future callers. I run a bluff because I feel my bet will be successful a sufficient percentage of the time for it to be the proper play in the given situation. In my opinion, you should always try to make the right play for your particular scenario, without thinking about the long-range effect of your action. Most players bluff too much, and rationalize their bad play by saying they are building a loose image to get action. If you play a lot of hands and do a lot of bluffing, please play in my games.

OMAHA BASICS

Omaha is an action-packed form of poker that blossomed into widespread popularity during the eighties. It is a community card game that employs four cards in the player's hand and five cards on the board. At the showdown, you must play precisely two cards from your hand and three cards from the board; no other combinations are allowed. As in hold'em, the dealer flops three boardcards simultaneously, and the last two boardcards are dealt one at a time. The player retains all four cards throughout the deal.

There are a number of misconceptions about Omaha floating around. The most common one is that a lot of starting hands can and should be played. The fact is Omaha follows the same strategy principles as all other forms of poker; it is a good policy to be fussy about one's weapons before entering battle. The myth of many playable hands at Omaha arises from the fact that the overlay of a good hand versus a mediocre one is not so great as in other forms of poker like hold'em. However, being at a less disadvantage than normal does not make playing borderline hands a good policy. You should be averaging about two hands played per round in a full game, over the course of an evening.

Another misconception about Omaha is that there is an inordinate amount of luck to the game. This myth comes from the fact that drawing hands beat made hands so often at Omaha. A set of trips is not as durable a hand as in regular hold'em. However, the skills that permit a good poker player to have an overlay in other forms of poker are also in demand at Omaha. If it were otherwise, great players such as Jack Keller, Berry Johnston, and Roger Moore would not be so enamored of the game. Frankly, I believe there is a greater need for skill at pot-limit Omaha than any other form of poker, especially in selection of starting hands and use of position.

To select the right starting hands, we must analyze what type of hands win pots, especially large pots. Here is what you are trying to build:

(1) **Big full houses**. The accent is on big. Omaha tends to produce a lot of multihanded pots, and five or six players in for the flop is not uncommon. When the board pairs, it usually takes a big full house to win. For example, when the board comes K-J-6, and a jack comes on fourth street, the guy who flopped a set of sixes usually winds up with egg on his face. The winning hand is usually K-K or K-J. This means big pairs and hands with high ranking cards are valuable, and smaller stuff is dangerous. A hand such as Q♠-Q♥-10♠-6♣ or K♥-J♠-10♠-8c is playable, but 9♥-9♠-7♥-4♣ or 9♦-8♦-6♣-3♥ will only get you into trouble.

(2) **Nut flushes**. Ace and another card on suit is a good Omaha holding. Don't play hands that have lower-ranking flushes working unless there is another reason to play besides being suited. A hand such as A♠-8♠-7♦-5♣ is playable, but beware of Q♠-J♦-7♠-5♦. The latter type hand I like to refer to as a "D.S.T. hand"—double-suited trash.

(3) **Nut straights.** The straight possibilities are enhanced by having four cards in the hand (instead of two) by a wider margin than is apparent at first thought. Even though there are only twice as many cards at Omaha (as opposed to hold'em), there are six times as many straight possibilities. In addition to A-B and C-D, we have A-C, A-D, B-C, and B-D. The way you build straights is to put the

emphasis on hands that have the cards close together in rank. Holdings of four-in-a-row such as 9-8-7-6, and one-gappers such as 9-8-7-5 and 9-8-6-5 are playable hands at Omaha, and excellent hands when the straight possibilities are enhanced by also having flush chances via being suited. Beware of having the gap at the high end of the holding. A hand like 9-7-6-5 is trouble, because the straights you are building by having the boardcard in the gap are usually not the nuts. If you want to make the nuts, you've got to build the nuts by proper selection of starting hands.

Americans normally learn hold'em before learning Omaha. In Britain, where pot-limit Omaha is rapidly becoming their national poker game, most Omaha players have omitted the intermediate step of first familiarizing themselves with the two-card game. While a foundation of hold'em is probably an asset, it also can lead to some mistakes. Here are some errors made by hold'em players who fail to make the proper adjustments when "graduating" to Omaha:

(1) **Checking their good hands.** It is a lot easier to draw out on somebody when you have four cards to work with. Obviously, it is giving away too much information to always bet right out with your good hands, but the tendency should be in that direction. Some players underestimate the danger of checking the nuts with flops such as 6-6-5 or 8-7-5. A small full house or small straight can easily be outrun, so charge a price for players who want to take a shot at you. At Omaha, if you bet the nuts and everyone folds, please don't take the pot with a look of disgust on your face. Smile and mentally thank Lady Luck.

The corollary to the danger of allowing free cards at Omaha is serious weakness shown by players who check to you. "Check" means "bet-and-take-it" more often than at hold'em. All the top pot-limit Omaha players pick up a lot of pots by using their money to run over people who have shown weakness.

(2) Overvaluing shaky holdings. There are many holdings that are good hands at hold'em, but poor hands at Omaha. On the flop, holdings filling this profile are an overpair, any two pair other than top two, small sets, and non-nut straight or flush draws. The hands run much bigger at Omaha, and any player failing to make a major adjustment on his scale of values is headed for trouble. Keep in mind those hands you want to build: the nut full house, the nut flush, and the nut straight.

(3) Underestimating the value of position. Position is not that important at limit Omaha—or limit poker in general—but it is critical at pot-limit Omaha. One point sometimes overlooked is that being in position is more important when drawing than when having a made hand. In early position with a made hand like a set, you usually just keep firing. A drawing hand, whether or not you hit it on fourth street, is much more strongly placed in late position. After all the cards are out, it is also very important to act last. Beware of over-valuing drawing type hands before the flop in early position at pot-limit play. A hand with a suited ace is much more likely to flop a draw than an actual flush, so prefer late position with this holding.

Nearly all major poker tournaments have a pot-limit Omaha event these days. I attribute part of the reason for my successful record at tournament events to the adjustments I make in my style of play. At tournaments, getting a hand cracked means a serious wound, and often a fatality. At a full table, I am even more cautious at initially getting involved than is the case at money games. However, I am more aggressive than usual in betting flops. There are several reasons for this. First, you have more heads-up situations in a tournament. Second, the better players won't call as often, because one mistake means they are out. (Tournament events allowing rebuys therefore have somewhat looser play, so bear in mind that you will get called more often in this type of tournament.) Third, since my starting hands are a little better, I hit the flop slightly more often. Fourth, each pot becomes very important to win, because it represents more in proportion to my stack than is normally the case at a money game. Fifth, the penalty for running into a big hand, even though it probably will be fatal, is not as great as in a money game, in proportion to what you are winning if the opponent folds. This is because of the high blind structure used for tournament play. In Omaha tournaments, especially on the betting round after the flop, fortune favors the bold.

Another adjustment you should make in tournament play is big pairs are more valuable. A hand with two aces, or two kings with an ace kicker, is worth more in a higher blind structure. A big raise before the flop usually indicates a big pair. At money play, it is a bigger liability to give away information about the nature of your hand by a preflop raise, because the money is deeper. If the money situation is such that you can get all-in with one bet on the flop, raising preflop on a big pair is more attractive. If there still is going to be a substantial amount of money left after you bet the flop, giving away vital information about your hand can be much more expensive. The opponent gets an extra bonus for out-flopping a big pair, so he can afford to gamble more before the flop. For this reason, a preflop raise in tournament play often wins the pot, but at money play much less so. An important factor in deciding whether to raise is the chance of winning the pot outright. Since this chance is very reasonable for a preflop raise at tournament play, it stands to reason that big pairs should be played more aggressively than normal when playing in a tournament.

Despite Omaha's surge in popularity, there are still a lot of players that prefer hold'em. In talking to many of these people, I get the idea that their biggest objection to Omaha—aside from unfamiliarity—is the vulnerability of their good hands to being overtaken. Two aces before the flop has a huge overlay at hold'em; much less so at Omaha. Flopping a set at hold'em makes a player feel like he has a gun that can't miss. At Omaha, the feeling of being protected is not nearly as strong.

What the players who favor heavy armament need to realize is the weaker players like to have a chance. As I mentioned before, playing bad hands is not as costly at Omaha. What game do you think the loose gooses who like to play every other hand are going to be attracted to more? If you want to make money at poker, you have got to play with the action-loving players. The action junkies don't like to be nutted every time a big pot develops, so they play games where the uphill slant of the road is not so steep. Omaha hold'em is the action game, so wake up and realize it's time to learn how to play it. Otherwise, you are likely to wind up like some of the American hold'em players at a memorable European tournament; on the rail watching the Omaha players get the money.

Omaha is the poker form that attracts the kind of people you want to gamble with. For more complete information about the game see my book "Omaha Holdem Poker."

148

RETURN TO STUD

I first learned how to play poker in 1950 from my mother, Marjorie Ciaffone. I was a child of nine, and we were living on Long Island, NY. She taught me draw, five-card stud, and seven-card stud. Five-card stud was a dead game, and draw not that popular. So at that time, the game of seven-card stud was considered the most important form of poker.

In the fifties, sixties, and seventies, I learned a lot of newer poker forms (some of which you likely never heard of nor will ever hear of in the future). But seven-card stud continued in the role of being the basic form of poker that beginners normally learn first.

I became quite bored with stud. Like many of you, I'm always on the lookout for something new. I am fortunate in having the ability to learn the strategy for a new poker form very quickly. So when a new game comes along, that's the first place I go. Everyone knew how to play stud, so I kind of looked down on the game as "beginner poker." Since becoming a poker professional in the late 70's, I have played very little stud, and usually it was as a filler when waiting for a hold'em or Omaha game that interested me.

When I became a proposition player at Hollywood Park Casino, one of the poker games I was required to play in was the $15-$30 limit seven-card stud game. The Hollywood Park Casino management worked hard to promote their stud poker games. About half my playing time was spent in the stud game (the other half being spent mostly at limit hold'em).

To my surprise, I started showing the same profit edge at stud as at hold'em. And I looked at the game through a new pair of eyes. After all, I learned a lot about poker in my 17 prior years as a pro. And this general knowledge could be applied to stud very well.

Let me talk about why I now don't mind playing seven-card stud and consider it to be a challenging form of poker.

RETURN TO STUD

(1) In California, the expansion of legal poker forms in 1987 has made hold'em the basic game of high poker that casino players learn first. Some of these hold'em players are now trying to learn stud, thus reversing the previous roles these games have had in other parts of the country such as the East Coast and Midwest. As stated earlier, I like the "new games."

(2) In a hold'em game, you get drop-ins that do not know hold'em very well. But in a stud game, you get drop-ins that do not know **poker** very well. These people are of course highly desirable opponents.

(3) As a prop player, I played in quite a few shorthanded games. At least for me, stud is a substantially better form of poker than hold'em for shorthanded play. You can get a better read on what the opponent has. This makes it harder for aggressive players to push you around. You also get a reasonable starting hand at stud more often. A lot of times in a shorthanded hold'em game, it seems like many of my opponents are throwing their money into the pot like they have good hands, while I seem to be looking at an unending procession of holdings such as 10-5, 9-3, 6-2, and so forth. And when this happens, even though you know the opponents are flying around on very light holdings, there is not much you can do about it without incurring an unacceptably high risk. I may earn a living at gambling, but this doesn't mean I'm looking to gamble. In fact, I think of myself as being in the risk **avoidance** business.

(4) There is a lot more to seven-card stud than I realized. It seems like I learned something new about the game nearly every day. For an example, there are some sophisticated uses for raises such as isolating on the weak player or knocking one of your opponents out of the pot even when you know the other one has you beaten. So I have found that there are a lot of fine points to the game where a good player can get the edge on a mediocre player.

(5) I feel that stud poker offers the player more control over his money than hold'em does. As an example, when the opponent puts that drawout on you, if he does it with an upcard, you often see what happened and have a chance to get away from your hand. At hold'em, when they make that second pair, the earliest you find out about it is when they raise. And there is so much bluffing at hold'em you don't know whether to believe that raise or not. Much of the time, the pot odds force you to call. All my really horror-show nights have been in the hold'em game, whereas in stud I've yet to lose as much as a grand.

So if you are thinking about playing some seven-card stud, give it a try. I did, and liked it. There is a lot more to the game than many players realize.

STEALING AT STUD

A player who reads poker advice should not simply follow that advice as if it were the Ten Commandments. Rather, the player needs to see how the ideas fit into his own reference framework. The ones that fit can be used, and the ones that don't can be ignored. This applies no matter how good or bad the person imparting the information may be. Poker advice is in this respect no different than any other advice you may receive.

I am going to present some ideas to you on seven-card stud. These ideas work for me. The ones that sound like they might fit your style and personality you can consider trying.

Seven-card stud high as played for decent-size stakes in a casino setting is played with an ante and a forced bet by the lowest upcard. At some point in a poker game you need to think about stealing the dead money that is in the pot at the start of a deal. I don't think there is some precise point in a deal where a player should go from not thinking about a steal at all to giving it serious consideration. The spectrum does not have that steep a transition in the space of only one seat. But if there were such a point, I know where it would be for me, at both hold'em and stud. When nobody has yet contested the pot, I start thinking about a steal when there are three or less players behind me yet to act.

The strategy of stealing the initial pot is even more important at stud than it is at hold'em. Look at the math involved at the $15-30 limit level. At hold'em, there is a $15 big blind and a $10 small blind, a total of $25 in blind money, and it costs $30 to try and steal it. At stud, there is in a full game $16 in antes plus the $5 force, a total of $21, and it costs $15 to try and steal it. So at stud, you risk less in proportion to the pot size; about 71% compared to 120% at hold'em. Furthermore, at stud you have one competitor, who is in for only a third of the bet. At hold'em, you have one person already in for half a bet, and another that is in for a third of the bet. This means you will get called substantially less often at stud than in hold'em. So if your starting hand at stud were dealt with all three cards facedown, the steal would be a more successful play at stud. Since you risk less, yet have a higher chance of success.

As we know, those starting cards at stud are not all facedown; one of them is faceup. And if you have the highest upcard among the remaining players, the possibility of a successful hijacking is of course even greater than if all the cards had been facedown. The chance of a successful steal is so good that most stud players, whether mediocre or expert, seem to raise and try to steal every time this situation arises.

I am one of those players who does not automatically steal in this situation where I have a big card up and three or less players to go through. My general philosophy of poker is to not do things automatically. Being predictable is not a poker virtue. So lets talk about a concrete situation.

Suppose I am in a newly started $15-30 limit sixhanded stud game and have the highest upcard, a king. The lowcard, a deuce, makes the $5 forced open, two players fold, and it is up to me. Most of the time, I will raise. So would anybody else that is not vying for the Caspar Milquetoast meekness award. But if I look down and find a dead deuce and another useless-looking trash card in the hole, I am going to fold. Once in a great while, I will even just call the forced bet, though this is considered to be a raise-or-fold situation. Yes, I probably could have stolen the pot. But by not stealing it in an obvious steal situation, some good things may happen as a result. Here are a couple of them.

First, there is a chance that I was getting called (or even raised). In such situations, it is nice to have ways to get lucky and make a legitimate hand. I think like a hold'em player, and a hold'em player would be cogitating, "I don't have much by way of outs here; only the other three aces."

Second, an image has been created in the minds of the other players. They will be thinking, "This guy doesn't like to put money in the pot without a hand; I'm not going to give him any action." Perhaps some of you readers have been inculcated with the idea that a successful poker player always wants to have the image of an Action Jackson, and actually be peddling the nuts. This philosophy

153

is okay, but there is another way to do things. If the opponents think you are a nuts-only player, and you are really a sneaky larcenous varmint, this is also a recipe for success. So after pusillanimously folding that king, you now have a tight image, which can be exploited. Maybe you can not only steal antes, but also some pots in later stages of play, where there is a much greater amount of money to be hijacked.

I do not want to give you the wrong impression. I do not start a session of poker saying to myself, "I am going to create a tight image and try to exploit it." Rather, I see how the play goes. If the cards are running all over me, I might try to look like I am giving a lot of action. But if situations come up where by making a solid sensible play, as opposed to the riskier play, I look like the Rock of Gibraltar, than I think the right thing to do is not be concerned about acquiring a tight image, but simply try to exploit it.

Maybe this is a good place to mention that the policy of not worrying if I get a tight image is available to me because I am playing in a public cardroom. If you are playing in a private game, having the reputation of a nuts player may incur the risk of not getting invited back. Home poker games have their own strategy rules.

If you make a couple of these "Why get involved?" folds, and the players are beginning to murmur, what is the best way to exploit this? Obviously, to hijack some pots. A favorite method of mine at stud is the fifth street steal. Why fifth street? Because it is the place where in the normal stud structure the limit doubles. Of course, I do not confine my larceny only to fifth street, but I think that is the place offering a good chance of success.

When you make a move on fourth street, the opponent can call cheaply, and he or she will often put you on a draw or mediocre hand. They think if you had a real big duke you would wait until the limit doubles.

When you make a move on sixth street, the opponent may feel that so much has already been invested that one may as well stay in for the duration and hope to draw out. And a move on seventh street seldom works; a lot of people call on hopeless hands just to see what you've got.

A nice thing about a move on fifth street is that is the place a player with a really big hand, like rolled up trips, often springs to life. A raise on fifth street is respected. And if the open cards hook up, there is the possibility of a complete hand such as a straight. It is hard for someone with only one pair to call a raise, because they can be drawing close to dead.

Refraining from stealing the antes in stud when you have the boss upcard but really bad holecards fits in well with my overall philosophy of poker. Stay out of pots on trash, don't become alarmed if you get a tight image, and steal pots when there is a decent amount of money in the middle to make it worth your while. Don't try from the start to cultivate a tight image, but if you get one, exploit it.

HIGH-LOW SPLIT STRATEGY

I can see by the frequent horrendous errors made in high-low split games that a lot of players must be unaware of fundamental split-pot strategy. Some players seem to like high-low poker because they think more starting hands are playable. They play all the hands that are their normal starters in a straight-high game, and of course a number of hands that aim primarily for low. The result is they are simply in too many pots on inadequate values.

The proper strategy for split-pot poker is to play approximately the same percentage of starting hands that are correct for that form of poker at straight high. Since a goodly number of your starting hands aim for low, it should be obvious that at least half the hands for high that would be adequate starters in a one-winner game must be mucked in a two-winner game. Just premium hands can be played for high.

The only hand that is a premium high hand in seven-card stud eight-or-better (other than those rare rolled-up trips) is an overpair to the other doorcards. Even a three-flush should be mucked unless it has a two-way potential by having at least a couple of cards toward a low qualifier.

Every once in a while, you still hear someone pontificating on high-low poker who offers this simple advice: "Play for low." That bit of wisdom was applicable to split-pot games of the seventies and earlier, when most games were played without a qualifier for low. When your heads-up opponent started with rolled-up kings, you automatically got half the pot (unless you were hard-luck enough to triple-pair) and were freerolling for the other half.

The reason high-low split became such a popular form of poker is directly attributable to the use of a qualifier of eight-or-better for low. Eight-or-better to qualify means that to win the low half you need five different cards of eight or under (an ace is okay for low). Otherwise, the best high hand wins the entire pot. This brought a sensible balance to the game, no longer overly emphasizing the low direction.

HIGH-LOW SPLIT STRATEGY

If I were asked to come up with a short epithet giving good split-pot strategy, it would be, "Aim for the whole pot." Every high hand has scoop potential, because the low draws may fail to make a qualifying hand. But some low-oriented hands have little high potential. A hand which aims only for low needs a lot of opponents to be playable. It is a miserable holding heads-up and weak in threehanded pots.

A starting hand with three low cards aims for the whole pot by meeting any of the following criteria:

(1) It contains an ace. This only helps if aces are live, of course. With an ace, you might improve to a pair of aces (or better), and thereby scoop a player who started with a big pair.

(2) It contains a three-straight. If there is no gap, such as 6-5-4 or 5-4-3, this is a premium hand. A one-gap hand such as 6-4-3 or 7-6-4 is usually quite good, but be alert as to how live is your middle card (a five in this case). A two-gap hand such as 7-6-3 is a borderline hand. And 7-3-2 doesn't reach; you need at least three opponents to play.

(3) It contains a three-flush. Again, see how live your suit is.

A starting hand often played in the wrong situation is a low pair with another low card, such as 5-5-3. This is a good starting hand heads-up, but weakens considerably in multihanded pots. The typical high-low pot has one player going for high and another going for low, with the third person being carved up. If one of your opponents has a big pair and the other has three cards of eight or under, you are substantially behind in both directions. Even if you get lucky and outdraw one opponent in a split-pot you will have been laying two-to-one on the money, which is obviously not what an underdog should be doing. A small pair with another low card begs to be folded in multihanded pots.

The most frequent mistake I see in high-low stud games is people continuing in the pot when they have started out going for low and buy a brick on fourth street. Seven-card stud is structured with two cheap betting rounds and three expensive betting rounds. There is seldom enough early money in the pot to warrant getting married to an underdog. If you bust out on fourth street, get out.

Another common mistake is overvaluing a big pair on fourth street. Naturally, if your opponent bricks up, everything is fine. But if your opponent catches another low card, he is in decent shape whether or not the card paired him. If that card is close in rank to his doorcard, you are probably in trouble. And if it also make him a two-flush as well as a two-straight, get out.

High-low split differs somewhat from one-winner poker in the type of skills that are emphasized. The skills of bluffing and reading the opponent are somewhat devalued, and there is more importance placed on technical soundness. A technically unsound player in a split-pot game is simply cannon fodder. To survive at high-low split eight-or-better, you must have good fundamentals. I don't care how well your play on the later betting rounds. You must build the right stuff from the start, or be a losing player.

OMAHA EIGHT-OR-BETTER

Limit Omaha high-low split with a qualifier of eight or better for low continues to grow in popularity. It is presently the most widely-played form of Omaha. One reason for this growth is there are still a lot of people who don't play it very well, so the games are attractive. In this chapter I will present you with some of my ideas on how to play the game.

Although I am the author of a book on Omaha, I do not have a lot of hours logged playing limit Omaha eight-or-better. I prefer pot-limit to limit play, and straight high to high-low split. Therefore, treat my advice on this subject with a questioning mind, and only use what seems logical to you. Of course, this is how you should be treating poker advice from any source.

As with other Omaha forms, there is a lot of doubt about which hands are playable. I think very few hands can be profitably played at this poker form.

An important thought in deciding which hands are playable should be, "If I catch a good flop, can I scoop the whole pot?" This idea of having scoop potential is vital to any kind of split-pot poker. Here are several hands frequently played that should usually be mucked:

(1) 9♥-8♥-7♣-6♦ — This is a good hand at straight high. At split, chances are if you help such low-ranking cards, someone will take half the pot with a low hand.

(2) A♠-10♣-7♥-2♦ — This hand has the important ace-deuce combination, but the lack of high-card strength and flush or straight potential makes it questionable. Playing such a hand in raised pots is definitely a no-no.

(3) K♠-5♦-3♠-2♣ – Your game plan is to flop an ace and have the nut low draw. Even if this longshot dream becomes reality, that ace is going to kill the value of your king for high, unless you are lucky enough to get the A♠ to come on the board, and then make a flush with it. Good luck; you are sure going to need it.

OMAHA EIGHT-OR-BETTER

Note that the listed hands are clearly bad bets in **shorthanded** pots. Splitting a heads-up or threehanded pot doesn't provide much profit. If there were a lot of players involved, the earn potential would be much greater. Therefore, dump these hands in early position, because you don't know whether a shorthanded or many-handed pot will develop on the deal. Hand number two may be played in late position if it looks like there will be a lot of players participating in the deal, and you can see the flop cheaply. There is a much better chance that nobody has an ace-deuce combination out against you if the pot is unraised, as this holding often forms the nucleus of a raising hand.

We examined some hands that need a large number of players in the pot; here is the other side of the coin. Have a look at this hand: A♠-A♥-10♦-7♣. Many split-pot players are overly aggressive with a pair of aces as part of their hand. Heads-up, it is a good hand that has scoop potential. In a sixhanded pot, for example, it is quite weak. The chances of winning high with two aces or low with A-7 are remote. Therefore, I think it is right to raise if you expect to sharply narrow the field. When a lot of people are committed to playing, it is not worth a raise, and might even be a fold under certain circumstances. For example, if someone opens with a raise and there are three callers, you have a real dog. You probably need to flop a set to have a good hand, and the deck is not ace-rich, to put it mildly.

There are many ideas that are important to playing Omaha high-low split correctly. In my opinion, the most important is to know whether you want a short-handed or many-handed pot. You should raise, call, or fold accordingly. The topflight Omaha eight-or-better player must fold a lot of superficially attractive hands because the pot is not developing according to his hand's requirements.

The best way to evaluate an Omaha eight-or-better starting hand is to analyze what you need to flop in order to have a good hand, and the likelihood of getting it. For example, look at your combination for low. A hand such as K-K-3-2 needs to flop an ace, but an ace kills your pair of kings for high. Therefore, the hand is a lot weaker than it looks.

OMAHA EIGHT-OR-BETTER

If your low combination is an ace and a little card, what flop do you need to have a draw at the nut low? With A-2, all you need is a couple of non-pairing low cards. With A-3, you need a deuce and another low card. With A-4, you need both a deuce **and** a three on the flop to be drawing at the nuts. These three holdings are actually wide apart from each other in value. Careful concrete analysis of what you need and how likely it is to get will help you get a clearer idea of relative hand-values.

WHAT IS BIG-BET POKER?

"Big-bet Poker" is the term referring to no-limit and pot-limit play that is used in most modern poker rulebooks. (Previously, there was no term for this purpose.) No-limit means just that; a player may bet as much as he has in front of him. Pot-limit means a player may bet up to the size of the pot.

Both forms of big-bet poker are always played "table stakes," meaning only money on the table is in play. A player who is faced with a wager larger then his own stack may of course call for the amount in front of him. Hollywood has in certain movies put forth the idea that a player could make a gigantic bet that his opponent would be required to call in its entirety or fold his hand. Many of my acquaintances from outside the poker world have asked me if a player could actually win a pot in this manner. I explain to them it is just another area where Hollywood promotes a colorful myth at the expense of the truth. It is possible at some point in the history of the human race a game was held under the "Hollywood Rule," but to my knowledge not in the past hundred years.

How does big-bet poker differ in character from limit poker? Here are some of the ways:

(1) A bet has a better chance of winning the pot by inducing everybody to fold.

(2) Position is more important. Instead of gaining or saving one bet, as in limit play, a player is often able to use his position to win the whole pot.

(3) Making good bluffs and picking off bluffs becomes critical to the game.

One would think the greater room for expertise in big-bet poker, with its intensified emphasis on skills such as exploitation of position, bold play, and accurately reading the opponent, would be obvious to all. It amazes me that so many good poker players stick exclusively to limit play, claiming there is too much luck at big-bet poker! The feature scaring them is the large sum of money that can be lost on one hand. They fear a big catastrophe. I think they are people who are basically afraid to gamble very much. If they would keep score by the month or the year, instead of by the session, perhaps a different path would be chosen.

Some people think no-limit hold'em is the form of poker used to determine the World Champion simply because the Binion family—whose Horseshoe Casino hosts the game—is from Texas. Fifty years from now, maybe the World Championship might be held in a different place, but the game will still be no-limit hold'em. Not only is the skill requirement high at that game, but the spectator appeal is greater than any other form of poker. (This is why my favorite game of Omaha will not ever be used to contest the World Championship. The skill factor is extremely high, but how will a TV audience be able to follow and understand the play?)

Is there a strategy to follow at big-bet poker to make one a successful player? My opinion is "yes." You bet; your opponent tries to guess whether your hand really contains the values being represented. Most of the time you win. Often, your opponent is suspicious of your bet, but has a very weak hand. Rather than taking the chance of raising and finding out his hunch was wrong, he throws his hand away. If he has a hand strong enough to call, the battle is by no means won for him. He might get blown out of the pot by another bet. You might get lucky and beat him with the next card. Usually the bettor has some cards he can hit and get lucky. Sometimes you actually get dealt a strong hand, and have some goodies to back up your strong outward posture. The bettor has way the best of it. The best no-limit players range in style from fairly aggressive to very aggressive. "Nut" players may not lose much, but they don't win much either.

I don't mean to give you the impression that aggressiveness will make you a big-bet poker winner all by itself. It is still necessary to operate from the sound base of good starting hands and pick your spots. Don't play every hand that you are dealt as if it is the nuts. Select your hands carefully, but play strongly when you do get involved. The ten most aggressive players in Las Vegas are all poker dealers, not professional players. An aggressive style can be carried to excess—especially by a drunk.

WHAT IS BIG-BET POKER?

Aggressiveness is especially important in tournament play. The use of an ante along with blinds is the reason. There is enough money out there to make it worthwhile to steal. You must not only steal the antes occasionally, but also resteal from other would-be thieves. Look at the men who have won the World Championship in the 1980's. Stu Ungar (1980, 1981), Jack Straus (1982), Jack Keller (1984), Bill Smith (1985) and Phil Hellmuth (1989) are five of the most aggressive players in the world. The other three, Tom McEvoy (1983), Berry Johnston (1986) and Johnny Chan (1987 & 1988) are less aggressive than the first five, but still much more aggressive than most players. It seems you must be either "highly aggressive" or "selectively aggressive" to win the World Championship.

Lesser tournaments are also usually won by somebody that believes chips must be put into action, not salted away for posterity. Tournament chips have no cash value except in great quantities. A ton of them is worth a lot, but a few pounds are worthless. It continually amazes me to see people in a tournament whose only goal is to last for several hours. The last thing I want to do during "prime time"—what I call the days during a major tournament—is kill most of the day in a tournament event and finish just out of the money. It is much better to get an "early out," and that fact shapes my strategy. Don't make "longevity bets" if you value your time. People say you should not take a race in a tournament when you are even money if you are the better player. I believe I'm the better player partly because my willingness to take a race at even money enables me to pick up some pots! Heads we win in the tournament, tails we win in the side games, but we don't waste valuable time.

Some low-limit poker players are reasonably successful despite the fact that they are not "people-persons." Reading opponents is not their long suit. They win because they are sound players. At big-bet poker, you simply must be good at reading opponents, because the human element is so much more important. At limit poker, when you misjudge someone, it usually costs you one bet. At big-bet poker, such an error can cost you all your chips. That is why we call this form "A People Game."

THE SKILL FACTOR

Which form of poker has the greater skill factor; limit poker or big-bet poker (pot-limit and no-limit poker)? Once in a great while you will come across an article in a poker publication—always written by a limit player—that would have you believe limit play is the more demanding form on skill and talent. According to the best players in the world at both forms, big-bet poker has a far greater element of skill. Let's listen to a couple of knowledgeable people.

Johnny Chan has won the title of World Champion two years in a row. That competition is of course held at no-limit hold'em, the form of poker two-time World Champion Doyle Brunson characterizes as "The Cadillac of Poker Games." Johnny Chan has also demonstrated sufficient qualities—by winning several million dollars—to be considered an authority on limit play as well. I talked to Johnny about comparing the skill factor between big-bet and limit play. Here is Johnny's answer to my question of whether he felt he had a bigger overlay (against the same quality of opponents) at limit hold'em or no-limit hold'em. "There is a lot of luck at limit hold'em; it is almost a hand-holding contest. There is no gamble to no-limit hold'em." Translating from Chinese, this means there is no gamble to no-limit hold'em when **he** plays it. His overlay at that poker form is so great that he wins nearly every session.

I also asked 1986 World Champion Berry Johnston to contrast limit poker with big-bet poker. Berry is superb at both forms. Berry said, "There is more play by far to pot-limit hold'em than limit hold'em." Berry also made the point that he prefers pot-limit to no-limit because players lean on the antes too much at no-limit, and this takes some of the play out of it.

One article knocking big-bet poker used an example of "Suppose in a multiway pot you flop the top pair (jacks) in early position; how do you play it?" The author intimated that this is a complicated problem at limit play, but straightforward at no-limit.

165

THE SKILL FACTOR

My opinion is this is not the most taxing poker problem ever invented, regardless of whether it is limit or no-limit. How far wrong could it be to simply bet your hand? There may be some exceptions, such as in a no-limit tournament when the money situation is such that you can check-raise habitual button bettor all-in. Normally, you bet. Frankly, let's skip the ABC stuff and see how we can make this "problem" a real problem.

What do you do when a tough player like Johnny Chan calls your jacks on the flop? At limit play I would simply bet on fourth street (assuming a blank comes) and see what happens. At no-limit I would be feeling very uncomfortable. Johnny will call a player with no hand and no draw if he thinks the guy will check and release on fourth street when holding only one pair. After all, the odds favor the bettor having only one pair. Johnny will also smooth-call you on the flop when he turns a set of trips, provided the board is raggedy. So what do you do when you get called?

One thing you can do against this type of player is become a "two-barrel man," a player who fires chips again on fourth street with only top pair. If Johnny finds this out, and the money is deep enough, he might call you again with nothing, and take the pot away from you on the end. A defense against this stuff is to check-raise on fourth after leading at the pot on the flop; this is obviously quite risky.

There is a lot to think about at no-limit poker. I don't claim there are more tough decisions than at limit, but the consequences of a bad decision are far worse. This means a good player has a substantially greater overlay on the other players because the amount of money riding on each decision is higher.

The interpretation of the words "skill factor" can be a matter of semantics. Let us compare Game A with Game B. In game A, there are ten million factors that must be taken into consideration when making a decision. If you get all ten million factors right, you have a five percent edge in the game. In game B, there are a mere million factors to be considered. However, if you get them all right, you have a twenty percent edge. Which game has the most skill? I think your answer would be the same as mine. "My decision is where to spend my time. The relevant aspect to making this decision is where I can make the most money, so I will play where my chance of winning is the greatest, in game B." I am certainly not willing to concede that limit hold'em is a more intricate poker form than big-bet poker, but even if it were, the uncontroversial truth is that a skillful player has a bigger overlay against average opponents at big-bet poker.

The author of that other article acknowledges that the expert big-bet player has a great edge over weak players, but says that, "No-limit is too easy to play well," and claims the big edge is only against weak competition. Frankly, this opinion is rubbish! The guys I make a living from at pot-limit Omaha are **far** better poker players on the average than the guys he makes a living from in limit hold'em. They have more poker experience, more tricky moves, and more aggressiveness. (Fortunately for me, they do not have more discipline. Most of them play quite well only until somebody puts a drawout on them.)

Limit poker is much more popular than big-bet poker. The reason is the "live ones" win fairly often at limit play, so they keep coming back. At big-bet poker they are doubly outgunned; the game is more difficult to play, and the caliber of competition is normally tougher as well. The "live ones" have a major role in determining where the rest of us play. It is much easier to find a limit game, but if you are lucky enough to locate a big-bet game, it figures to be the more profitable place to spend your time. This is the real truth about limit vs. big-bet poker.

HOW MUCH TO BET

At limit poker the amount you can bet is usually fixed, relieving the player of a sometimes difficult choice. At pot-limit play the bet size is an important decision. What are the main factors that a player considers when deciding how much to bet?

An article by another author discussed this point. He examined this question from a strictly technical view, and concluded that it would be correct to bet the full size of the pot unless you have something approaching a lock. The obvious drawback to this strategy in a real game is your opponents would quickly detect what you were doing and adopt the appropriate counter-strategy.

I remember playing in a pot-limit Omaha game back in the 80's with a former World Champion whose policy seemed to be to bet the full pot size in all situations. (At Omaha a lot of top players do this because big drawing hands are so common.) A deal arose where the WC made a big preflop reraise, marking him with a likely pair of aces. His lone opponent in the pot was a rookie who had just gotten into our game. The flop came down ace-rag-rag with a couple of hearts. The rookie had to act first and checked. There was about $1500 in the pot. To the amazement of us veterans, the WC bet only $800 instead of his habitual full size of the pot. We all knew exactly what had happened. The WC had managed to flop the nut flush draw to go with his three aces, and was making a cheap bet to entice his opponent to draw at the flush. The rookie, unfortunate enough to be holding a king-high flush draw, was oblivious and called. On fourth street a heart popped off the deck. Like a scripted play, the rookie bet, got moved in, and lost all his money (over five grand) to the nut flush. He learned the hard way to beware of a Greek gift in a pot-limit game. Here the WC knew his opponent was inexperienced enough to fall into the trap. Most of the time a simplistic strategy of betting the whole pot unless your hand is huge enough to offer opponents a more enticing price is too crude to be an effective betting policy.

Sometimes the amount you select to bet can be chosen for purely psychological reasons. Here is a hand I played in a no-limit hold'em money game about eight years ago. In an unraised pot, I was in last position against the big blind and an early caller. The flop came Q-9-6 of different suits. There was $90 in the pot. My opponents both checked. I moved all my money in, over $800. The player in the big blind was T. J. Cloutier, who is a better no-limit player than I am or you are. T. J. had been playing poker with me for ten years, and had never seen me make a bet that far out-of-line into a small pot before. He held a queen in his hand, giving him top pair, and curiosity got the best of him. He called, no doubt thinking I was screwing around with a straight draw. My three nines held up. Even a top player can be fooled once in a while.

Even though there can be special occasions every so often, you need to have a regular strategy to use, because a pot-limit player gets to play against many familiar faces. You need a plan of selecting your bet size that is technically sound, yet deceptive enough to work against people who play with you on a steady basis. Let me tell you what I do and see if you like it.

The first thing we need to do is draw a distinction between hold'em and Omaha. At Omaha you need to bet the full pot size more often, because the drawing hands run much bigger. And at that game when the straight or flush card comes, it seems to always actually make that hand for your opponent.

For me, by far the most important factor in deciding how much money to bet is the texture of the flop. If the flop consists of three different suits with no possible straight draw, I don't need to bet much to protect my hand. I'm talking about the flops of K-8-3, K-8-2, K-7-2, and Q-7-2. Against as weak a hand as top pair, an opponent who is behind will have no more than six outs at hold'em. (Note that eleven outs are possible at Omaha, because you can have a pair with three kickers.) My typical bet at hold'em in this situation is one-third to two-thirds the pot size. If the preflop betting appears sufficient to remove players holding small cards such as 6-5 or 5-4, then you can treat flops like Q-7-4 or J-6-3 the same as a totally raggedy flop.

THE SKILL FACTOR

These ragged flops are of course a tempting target for a steal, especially at pot-limit poker. Whether I have top set, top pair, or a cold bluff, my bet size is the same. That way, my bet size does not reveal any information about my hand. A theory has been put forward under the name "Cappelletti's Assumption" that betting half the pot size would result in that bet winning immediately half as often as a bet of the full size of the pot. I believe this assumption was made simply for the purpose of making mathematical computations easier. My experience is that with ragged flops, a bet of half the pot will win immediately almost as often as a bet of the whole pot. This means a bluff of this size is quite an attractive proposition, because you are getting laid two-to-one odds. Assuming that you are betting the same amount on your strong hands and don't overwork the play, you should show a nice profit on your thievery. The astute reader may wish to point out that you are making less money on your good hands. There is no such thing as a free lunch. I hold many more bad hands than good hands. Perhaps those of you who habitually hold big hands may wish to make larger bets in this situation. I can tell you only what works for me.

The other layout of cards where you do not have much fear of a draw is when the opponent is probably drawing at a loser. This usually occurs when the board is paired and you are fortunate enough to have a full house. I find at hold'em many times a player is willing to draw at a straight or a flush when the board is paired. So at hold'em I normally bet the full size of the pot here, whether or not I have a full house. But at Omaha they have more respect when the board is paired. A bet of about half the pot is sufficient to pry someone loose from a draw in most cases, and that is the bet size I recommend.

In most other situations I am going to bet the full size of the pot, or pretty close to it. Even when a would-be caller doesn't seem to have enough outs to make a call seem mathematically correct, you often get played with anyway. The implied odds usually favor the caller, because completing a draw gives that player a chance to milk some extra money. And there is always the possibility of stealing the cookies later on. So you normally want to make it as hard as possible for the opposition to remain in the pot.

How many top big-bet poker players use this system of letting the texture of the flop dictate the size of the bet? Nearly all of them do, with their own modifications inside the overall framework. Perhaps you should too.

OVERBETTING THE POT

A nice feature of big-bet poker is you have the option of choosing how much to bet, rather than having the amount fixed by the betting structure. The flexible bet size lets you tailor your bet to the situation. Of course, this also conveys information about your hand. When my opponent bets, a big portion of my read on his holding is determined by how much he bet.

This is a good time to mention that one great advantage of a no-limit betting structure, as opposed to pot-limit, is that you do not have the "dealer interference" problem. Back in the early eighties, it was customary in pot-limit games to have the dealer announce the pot size after each betting round. When a player made the maximum bet, you never knew if he has done this simply because the dealer had encouraged him to do so. The dealer had deprived you of important information to which you were entitled. This horrific practice was finally abandoned after I and a number of other poker pros put on an intensive lobbying effort against it.

For Omaha, pot-limit betting is the preferred structure. But for hold'em, most of us like no-limit. Besides eliminating the big-mouth dealer problem, no-limit betting has other advantages. First, it enables you to pick up a lot of pots by a big preflop raise. Second, it lets you play a drawing hand more aggressively. Let's talk about these situations where you should overbet the pot.

Suppose you hold a hand such as A-J offsuit in the big blind. Pretend the stakes are a ten-dollar blind no-limit game and five people limp in to call you. If you decide to raise, it is clearly correct to raise to a total of $80 or $100 rather than a wimpy pot-size raise of $60. Your goal with this type of hand is to win it right there, not to simply build a big pot. Anyone who wants to build a big pot when holding an A-J offsuit in early position needs to visit a poker shrink for psychiatric treatment.

This is but one example of a situation where overbetting the pot is done out of weakness rather than strength. To keep would-be callers or raisers away, you need to vary your game.

OVERBETTING THE POT

Every once in a while with this type of betting, show up with K-K instead of a semi-steal.

Another good place to overbet the pot is when raising right after the flop out-of-position with a drawing hand. For example, suppose the flop comes K♠-9♥-8♥, and you hold K♥-J♥. this gives you top pair with a jack kicker, plus a king-high flush draw. You check and someone bets. It is unclear whether you have the best made hand. It is also far from certain that your draw is to the nuts, as many players will lead at the pot with an ace-high flush draw. What's clear is that you have a good hand which cannot be overlaid in both departments (made hand and drawing hand) by a single opponent. **Warning**: avoid a big threeway pot with this type of hand. The right play is to scoot the loot all-in. This is also the way you should play a set with this type of flop in front position. If you do not raise all-in, but simply create a big pot, you will be out-of-position on fourth street, and may well be confronted with a tough decision, whether holding either the K♥-J♥ or the 9-9.

Another situation where you should overbet the pot comes up quite often, especially in tournament play. If a normal-size raise would only put you about halfway in, it is superior to simply bet your entire stack. For example, you hold ace-rag suited, and have about a grand in front of you. The blinds are $75 and $150 in a no-limit tournament. You are in late position, and want to open for a raise and win the blind money. (Nobody else is in yet.) A pot-size raise would be to make it about $500 to go, but this is the wrong play. If someone put you all-in for your remaining $500, you would have to call and try and draw out, because half your stack is already out there. The proper play is to move in your entire stack at the start. This way, you put the maximum amount of pressure on your opponents. Note that if you had started the deal with two grand, you are not committed to the pot, so it is improper to open for your entire stack.

Most of the time when you bet, you would rather win the pot right there. Why give the opponent a chance to call cheaply and then break you? No-limit play gives you the **privilege** of overbetting the pot. Know when to use it.

POSITION

Position is far more important at big-bet poker (pot-limit and no-limit play) than at limit poker. Limit poker players usually use their position to win an additional bet or save a bet. Big-bet players can often use their position to win the whole pot. Even if you only gain or save one bet on a hand of big-bet poker, that wager is usually about the size of the pot.

People associate positional advantage in a hold'em game with their location relative to the button. The player on the button has the privilege of last action on three betting rounds: the flop, fourth street, and fifth street. Position is obviously more valuable if it can be exercised on all three of those betting rounds. Sometimes you or your opponent will run out of chips and be all-in on the flop or fourth street, which of course nullifies the positional advantage on subsequent betting rounds. This obvious fact has some crucial ramifications on play, as follows:

First, the deeper the money, the more important it becomes to have good position. Naturally, more money is at stake, but the point I am stressing is deeper money means a lower likelihood of someone getting all-in and depriving the person with position from using it throughout the hand.

Second, pot-limit play puts more emphasis on good position than no-limit play, because the player out-of-position cannot get all-in (and thus, nullify his positional disadvantage) as easily. It is particularly important at pot-limit to have good position on your drawing hands, because it is hard to "scoot" all your money in on the flop without a lot of help from your opponent. You do not want to have half your money in and be out of position on fourth street. If your opponent puts you on a draw, he will get away from his hand if you hit, and set you all-in if you miss. Naturally, your action in front of him is likely to reveal the nature of your hand.

Third, good position is usually less important in tournament play than in money play. At a tournament event, chips are not as deep in relation to the size of the blinds as they would normally be in a money game with the same blind structure. You often have position only on the flop because someone will be all-in. Some players would actually rather act first in a number of situations. By having the right of "first bluff," they get a chance to avoid a showdown that would have ensued had their opponent acted first and bet. Another difference in tournament play is the frequent use of an ante to supplement the blind structure. The larger pot-size means players often get involved without holding sound values. In such an environment the opportunity for "first bluff" is not to be sneered at.

We can rank the different forms of big-bet poker in the order of importance of good position. (Remember that position is important in all of them, and we are making only a relative comparison). The three games most often played at big-bet poker are lowball, hold'em, and Omaha. Lowball, with only two betting rounds, clearly gives less opportunity to utilize position than hold'em. Contrasting hold'em with Omaha, it is much more dangerous to give an opponent with a four-card hand a free card by checking. The pressure on a person who thinks he has the better hand to protect it by betting is very great at Omaha. When the opponent checks to you, he is likely to be surrendering if you bet. Since there is less deception when an opponent checks to you at Omaha, your positional advantage is worth more. If the Omaha game is being played at high-low split, position may be even more critical than in Omaha straight high. This may not necessarily hold true on the flop, but position on fourth and fifth street is vital in a split-pot game. You get to see whether there is a possible low— Omaha split is normally played with a qualifier for low—and how your opponent reacts to its presence or absence.

At hold'em, position relative to a player who has shown strength and is likely to bet on the next round can be more important than position relative to the button. It is better to be last to act in practice than in theory. For example, if you are in the big blind and a solid player opens with a raise, you are better placed than the people who call in late position. On the flop you can check and will be last to act if the raiser bets as expected. Of course, you

POSITION

will be first to act on fourth and fifth streets, but last-action on the flop rates to be more important.

Naturally, you do not have to check. You can put a lot of pressure on the raiser by betting through him. If he has a marginal hand, he will not relish putting chips in the pot with some unknown quantities behind him. He may suspicious you are stealing because you did not wait for him to bet and put the other players in the middle. But he knows that even if he guesses correctly that you are stealing, this knowledge may just get him into trouble, because he still needs to get by the other players in the pot to capture the cheese. If he has a good hand, he may be afraid to just call and let someone pick off a card at a relatively cheap price. Your bet puts him to a tough test, whatever his hand.

Let's look at a situation where you are on the button and the player on your right raises before the flop. Your normally good position has just fallen down like Baby Jessica. For example, suppose there are a couple of other callers and four of you take the flop. If the first two players check the flop and the raiser bets, you have been put in the middle. You may have him beat and get ambushed by one of the other players. If the raiser fails to bet, you cannot try to bet-and-take-it with any assurance of success. The raiser probably does not have enough to call, but one of the other players might have checked a good hand, expecting the raiser to bet. He will bag you instead! Had the raiser been first to act instead of third, and the field checked to you, there would have been a lot better chance that the coast was clear for a hijacking. Note that position relative to the raiser is much more important at hold'em than Omaha because it is much more likely that the raiser will bet the flop in the two-card game. Omaha players like to have a good piece of the flop before leading out with a bet into the field.

Good position may seem more important as the number of players involved in the pot increases. After all, the more players are in the hand, the more you have position on. This argument sounds plausible, but it is actually misleading. If seven people checked to you, would you try to steal the pot? Of course not. My favorite number of players to maximize the positional advantage of last-action is three. There are only two opponents to get through, so it is not that difficult to steal the pot. After three, the best numbers may be four, then two. If there is not that chance to steal, your position is worth much less. Position is nice when heads-up, but "check" often does not roll out the red carpet to walk off with the pot. Good players are willing to check-raise heads-up when they have nothing, but are much less likely to use this move in a three-way or four-way pot. A player is also less willing to check a good hand and allow a possible free card if he has more than one opponent.

Good position is useful in any form of poker. It is vitally important at big-bet poker. Hall-of-Famer Doyle Brunson claims he could beat a no-limit hold'em game without ever looking at his cards if he had position all night and the other players were not aware he was playing "in the dark." I believe him.

WHERE'S HE FROM?

"Where's he from?" This is a question you should ask yourself in a hold'em game. When attempting to gauge your opponent's probable strength after the flop, you must consider how many people stayed for the flop. Was he your only opponent? If so, then he would have to be quite lucky to hit a big hand. But if not, then he figures to be the best hand that was hit by the group of people that stayed for the flop. The best poker player in New York figures to be more skillful than the best poker player in Podunk, because he is the best from a much larger group of people. The bigger the group, the better the hand figures to be. Here is an obvious example of this principle at work.

Here is an example of what I mean. You pick up a pair of pocket aces in a no-limit hold'em game. You open for a raise and get called. The flop is 9-8-3 of different suits, which does not improve your hand. You bet the flop and get raised. There is still a fair amount of money left. Do you reraise all-in or fold? (To call out-of-position does not look like a reasonable alternative to me.)

This is a tough problem whose proper answer depends on who is your opponent, whether he bluffs much, and a host of other factors. My point is that a very important consideration should be how many people stayed for the flop. (I deliberately did not mention this when posing the problem to you.)

Were you heads-up? If so, my inclination would be to go ahead and take a race. It's not that easy for a single player to out-flop a pair of aces. Besides, a one-on-one situation seems to bring out a certain macho element of who's over who on the pecking order.

With multiple opponents, the picture changes. Suppose three people had called your preflop raise. Now you are presumably up against the best-out-of-three from the hands arrayed against you. Therefore, it is a much riskier proposition for you to reraise all-in.

To make this perfectly obvious, suppose it is a ninehanded game and everybody had called a preflop raise. In this situation I would probably be afraid even to bet the flop holding only one pair! The percentages favor someone in the field can now beat a pair, even though that pair is aces. With each additional opponent, the odds on your aces holding up are substantially shortened.

I remember an incident that happened in a poker game in the early eighties. The game was no-limit hold'em. Six people took the flop, which was a jack and a couple of rags. The first player to act was Louisiana Charlie; he made a pot-size bet. Everybody folded except the last player, who held a K-J, giving him top pair with a good kicker. Charlie had the reputation of a highly aggressive player, which he fully deserved. The last man against him, an experienced but not topflight no-limit player, went into a long huddle. Was Charlie bluffing again? Finally, the man went all-in with a raise. His own short stack and Charlie's reputation as a thief made him decide to play.

Of course, K-J was not the superior hand. I forget now what Charlie held, but it was a long ways out in front of that K-J, and stayed there.

I feel this is clearly a fold against virtually anybody. Aside from the fact that people ordinarily are not bluffing—or even holding a marginal hand—when they lead out in first position into five opponents, there is another factor. **Someone** rated to hit a good hand when six people saw the flop. Since nobody else had helped, it seems reasonable to assume that Charlie did.

The next time a large group of people take the flop, and a fast player (or anyone else) bets, I think it is prudent to assume he has a good hand. Somebody figured to hit the flop. If that person happens to be the fast player, that is still no reason to give him a donation.

Anytime you have to make a decision on the flop, ask yourself about the bettor, "Where did he come from?" If he came out of a large field of participants, watch out! This also applies when a bunch of players check to the button, who now bets. The button position has the well-deserved reputation for being a steal position. If nobody shows any strength, the coast may look clear for a hijacking. But there is a whale of a difference between two people checking to the button, who now bets, and four or more people checking to the button, who now bets. In the latter case, there is a fine chance the player has a real hand. So even if the button is someone who is a habitual thief, you still have to be careful.

The converse is also true. When only you and one other player stay for the flop, the odds say that neither one of you will hit something special. Therefore, there are three reasons why your opponent does not figure to be loaded for bear when he bets:

(1) The odds were initially against him helping.

(2) The odds were also against you helping. The other player of course knows this (or at least senses it), and is therefore more likely to try and take the pot away from you.

(3) If he did turn a big hand, he is more likely than normal to feign weakness when heads-up, because he doesn't put you on a hand that can take pressure.

FLOPPING THE NUTS

It is a sweet feeling at poker to hold "the nuts," the best possible hand at that point. A poker saying about the nuts is, "It's more important to get it then how you bet it." Nevertheless, betting any class of hands properly will help your finances.

In the following quiz, the game is pot-limit Omaha. Assume you and all the other players start the deal with $1,000. Each problem has you holding the nuts. The "correct" answer is the play that I feel is the percentage action on the hand. Keep in mind that you need to vary how you play the nuts, especially against a lineup of players that you face on a regular basis. Therefore, the answer is the one that I feel should be used more than half the time, but certainly not all the time.

(1) You hold A♠-J♠-10♥-2♥ on the button. The flop gives you the nut flush; K♠-Q♠-3♠. There is $100 in the pot. Four other players take the flop, and they all check it to you. Do you check or bet?

Answer: Bet. Having two big cards like a king and queen come on the flop makes it far more likely than usual that someone has flopped a set, because big pairs are hardly ever folded before the flop in unraised pots. Bet and charge your opponents a price for drawing. It is also possible that someone will mistake your button bet for a steal and incorrectly put a play on you.

(2) You hold 9♠-8♠-6♥-5♣. The flop is J♦-10♦-7♣, giving you the nut straight. As before, there is $100 in the pot. You are the second of 5 players to act after the flop. The first player leads out for the size of the pot. Do you raise, call, or fold?

Answer: Fold. Hey, I'm serious. Fold. You have the worst possible position, with a bet coming through you, and three players behind you. The better undoubtedly has a strong holding to bet that texture

FLOPPING THE NUTS

flop into four other people. He may well have the nuts **and** a freerolling flush or bigger straight draw. He could have a set and a flush draw, or some other kind of big draw. A threeway pot leaves you in terrible shape, likely tied right now and no way to improve. There are 32 cards (out of 45) on the next street that leave you without the nuts anymore, and there are **two** cards to come. If you are emotionally incapable of folding the nuts, forget about pot-limit Omaha and go back to hold'em, where you possibly have a chance.

(3) You hold K♠-K♣-3♠-3♣ on the button. The flop comes down K♦-7♣-2♠, giving you top set, with no possibility of a flush or straight being completed on the next card. You are on the button, and have raised preflop, with 4 callers. There is $750 in the pot; you have another $850 left. Everyone checks the flop to you; do you check or bet?

Answer: It is clear that you should bet. If you give a free card and "trap" someone into betting the next round, the money situation is unfavorable. You will only be able to go all-in for a little more, and therefore can neither bet a drawing hand out of the pot nor charge him a big price to draw. If everybody had at least three grand left, checking would be much more reasonable, as you then have enough money to raise meaningfully if someone bets. To understand the risk of a free card, picture the 6♣ coming on fourth street. With that 7♣ on the board from the flop, a potentially big draw could be created. Someone with a flush-draw and a 9-8 straight-draw combination is a big threat. If that person also had a 5, giving them a wraparound and flush-draw, they would actually be a slight favorite over your three kings even with only one card to come. It should be noted that the right play when flopping a set of kings with this texture flop at hold'em is certainly to check, but this is an **Omaha** problem. A drawing hand at Omaha can be a monster, so don't give anyone the opportunity to pick up a draw just because you have a set.

(4) You hold A♦-K♠-Q♠-5♦. The flop is K♣-K♦-Q♣. Five people stay for the flop; you are first to act. Do you check or bet?

Answer: Check. It is unlikely anybody has much, and most unlikely that anybody will draw out on you. This is about how much hand you need at Omaha to make checking a clearly correct play.

Many people seem to play mechanically when they flop or make the nuts. Their first reaction is to check. At any form of poker, you should vary how you play the nuts, but particularly at pot-limit. It may well be technically correct to bet. This is especially likely to be true at a game such as Omaha where big draws abound.

BETTING WITHOUT ANY OUTS

Hold'em and Omaha players use the term "outs" referring to board-cards that will win the pot for you. For example, if you hold a flush-draw and are up against an overpair with one card to come, your hold'em hand will have nine outs (or eight if the opponent has a card of your flush-suit).

Especially for big-bet poker, we are warned by poker writers to have outs when making a play for the pot. This way, we have two chances to win. The opponent may fold, or we may hit one of our out-cards and win the pot legitimately. This certainly makes sense. Since we are not going to be betting at the pot every time we are a contender, it seems wise to do so when we have that double chance to win.

However, like most good rules, there are some exceptions. Situations can arise where we need to break this normally good rule in order to take maximum advantage of opportunities that can arise in a poker game. This discussion will focus on a couple of those situations.

The first thing we should realize is that having outs is far more important when going all-in than when simply making a play for the pot. Look at this situation. Suppose you have one opponent, and he is a tough player. The game is no-limit hold'em, and there is a thousand dollars in the pot. You and your opponent each have two thousand dollars left. If you are contemplating betting a grand to try and win the pot, is it a big advantage to have a flush-draw rather than nothing?

If you bet a grand and your opponent simply calls, that would make three grand in the pot and only one grand left in each player's stack. An astute opponent who has only a simple straight-draw or flush-draw is not going to call you with just one card to come. He would be getting insufficient odds to justify a call.

If the opponent has a made hand and opts to continue contending the pot, he is once again not going to call. He is going to move all-in in case you are drawing. So either way, it is unlikely the opponent will simply call your thousand-dollar bet.

If your opponent raises that other grand when you bet, does it help to have a flush-draw? You are now being laid four thousand to a thousand, but 4-1 odds with only one card to come means that you are not quite getting the right price to justify a call.

As you see, in the situation we hypothesized, having an 8-out or 9-out draw was not helpful. Of course, poker players do not always behave in a matter that logic dictates. It is possible that an opponent might simply call (perhaps we misjudged his astuteness), in which case it would be nice to have a way to get lucky. My point is to illustrate that a bet of half your stack is less in need of outs than an all-in bet.

Another poker admonition, especially for no-limit players, is to avoid drawing to a straight or flush when the board is paired. (This is another good rule that needs breaking on occasion.) What implication does this have for a rule-bound player when the board is paired? If he cannot bet unless having outs, and cannot bet a draw when the board is paired, when can he bet? If he follows the two rules we mentioned, I guess he can only bet when he thinks his hand is the best.

Certainly it is a violation of common sense to never bluff at the pot when there is a pair on the board. The fact of the matter is bluffing at the pot when the board is paired is one of the more desirable situations for a hijacking. There are fewer card combinations that would make an opponent interested in the pot. He also has to face the possibility that he is drawing dead when trying to make a straight or a flush.

A good player knows when to break the rules. There are times when it is necessary to bet at the pot without any outs. Your skill will improve if you start tuning in to these opportunities. "Never bet without an out" is a beginners rule. The expert must be aware of when to break it, although he does so sparingly.

WALKIN' BACK TO HOUSTON

The hold'em hand A-K is the most powerful starting hand among unpaired cards, and is valued higher than most pairs. This has caused it to acquire some nicknames. Limit players often call A-K "Big Slick," paying tribute to its power at that form of poker. However, the no-limit hold'em players from Texas have a colorful name for A-K that is much less flattering. They sometimes call it "Walkin' Back to Houston." The implication is no-limit players who regularly put a large amount of chips into the post on this holding will be lucky to have gas money left in their pockets.

There are clearcut differences in hand evaluation between limit and no-limit hold'em play. For example, flopping top pair is a worthy goal at limit play. At no-limit play, when there is a lot of money on the table in proportion to the blinds, top pair can often cost you more than you can win with it. If big money goes into the pot, the only thing your top pair can beat is a draw. The goal in no-limit is to build a hand that can double up your whole stack. Therefore, big unsuited cards such as A-K, A-Q, A-J, and K-Q are worth substantially less at no-limit poker. Such cards are mainly useful for building top pair, which should not be your goal when the money is deep. Conversely, intermediate pairs are worth more at no-limit, because flopping a set has a bigger bonus at that form of poker. Middle set is the typical hand for doubling through an opponent.

Actually, A-K is a better hand than an intermediate pair even at no-limit play if there is not much money on the table in relation to the size of the blinds. This condition exists in satellite tournaments and one-day events, which are by far the most common type of contests at no-limit play. This is why most no-limit **tournament** players view A-K much the same as limit players.

However, no-limit **money** players (at least the more successful ones) look upon A-K with a certain amount of contempt. They know what happens when you put too much money into the pot before the flop without holding a big pair.

Let's talk about some cash-game situations at no-limit hold'em where A-K is often played too strongly. We will assume the game is being played with a blind structure of $25 and $50, and each player starts with ten grand. This is the structure used at the first level for the World Championship no-limit hold 'em tournament. This four-day event, unlike most tournaments, starts out with a blind structure so low for the amount of money in front of you that a cash-game strategy is more appropriate at the early stages.

Suppose you raise the $50 blind to $250, and someone reraises the pot to a total of $1000. What should you do? If that grand had been an all-in bet, as in an average tournament, I would call. Most of the time the opponent has Q-Q or weaker, in which case the pot odds make the call correct, as you are only a slight underdog to such a hand. On your good days you run into hands such as A-Q or A-J, making you a solid favorite (better than 2-1).

However, when this type of raise is made against you when there is still a freightload of dough remaining to be bet, it is seldom done on hands like A-Q or 9-9. More likely, you are dueling with a big pair. Calling this type of reraise with A-K is asking to get broke. Most of the time, the caller is better off flopping blanks than catching a king—or maybe even an ace. When the money is deep, do not call a reraise with A-K.

At limit play, raising on A-K is considered the normal reaction. To not raise is something you do only to vary your play. It's practically sandbagging. I probably raise the pot over eighty percent of the time that I start with A-K in a full $20-40 limit hold'em game.

Let me tell you that raising on A-K in a no-limit cash-game is by no means automatic. Frankly, I probably just call about as often as I raise. Particularly, I think raising in middle position against one opponent who has called the blind up front is a risky proposition. If that person is a loose player that you want to isolate into a heads-up pot, go ahead and raise. But if that player is a solid type, why try to get heads-up? Remember that if A-K is not the best hand before the flop, you want a volume pot, since it is about 2-1 against flopping a pair.

WALKIN' BACK TO HOUSTON

I would like to take time here to point out that the nut flush-draw is even more powerful at no-limit than limit play. If someone else makes a flush in your suit, this is a potential double-up situation. Therefore, A-K suited is not to be treated the same way as A-K offsuit. Even so, beware of calling reraises even when suited.

Not all forms of hold 'em are alike. At a no-limit game with deep money, don't get too enamored of A-K. If you regularly put all your chips into the pot on this hand, the only thing that will keep you from walkin' back to Houston broke will be being from someplace else!

INSIDE MY HEAD

I am going to tell you about eight hands that I played in a typical pot-limit Omaha session very recently. Many people are hungry to know the thinking process of a poker pro when he plays a pot. This article will give you a glimpse of the reasoning behind every-day decisions similar to those faced by a pot-limit or no-limit player in an average session. Even if you are strictly a limit player, perhaps you will still find some entertainment and a helpful hint.

I enter a well-known Las Vegas cardroom and find my pot-limit Omaha game is in progress with precisely one seat open, so I already feel lucky. The game has a $1-$2-$5 blind. I take the seat and buy for three hundred dollars worth of chips.

Hand #1—The first hand that I get heavily involved in a pot with is A♥-K♥-Q♣-4♥. The flop that appears is quite a helpful one for my hand: A♣-10♥-5♥. I have top pair, a possible belly straight, and the nut flush draw. I bet $30 and get one call, from a player who previously checked. He is a youthful fellow who I know to be a local and have seen fairly often. The fourth street card is the 4♦, which creates a possible straight on board and makes me two pair. Surprisingly, my opponent leads right out for $60. I have far too much hand to fold, so the choice is between calling and raising. I doubt that my hand is good at this point, and it is unlikely an all-in raise would make my opponent fold, so I just call. The last card is the 10♠, pairing the board. My opponent checks quickly. Most people with my hand would check and see if it is any good, but I want to give my opponent a problem if he has a straight, so I make an aggressive $100 bet. My opponent makes an easy call and turns over a pair of fives in the hole; he had flopped a set and filled when the board paired on the end. My over-aggressive betting has gotten me off to a bad start. I have been completely outplayed and lost over half my buy-in.

Hand #2—A little while later I have made a slight financial comeback, and pick up A♦-5♦-4♠-4♣ on the button. I put in $5 to call, along with several callers in front of me. One of the blinds makes a small raise to $15 and we all call. The flop comes down 10♦-8♥-3♦, so I have the nut flush draw. A player in middle position bets $80. It is a common mistake to raise all-in when you only have another $100; a player strong enough to bet into five opponents isn't going to fold for a Franklin, so you usually want to give others an opportunity to play when you have the nut flush draw. I call—folding would also have been reasonable—and to my surprise Don, a player who previously checked, puts in a big raise. The original bettor folds his hand, and I call for what chips I have left. He holds the Q♠-J♣-9♦-7♦, a wraparound straight and a flush draw, so my pair of fours is the best hand at this point! He would have been a favorite against a set, but is only about even money against my hand. I buy a diamond on the last card and win a nice pot.

Hand #3—I'm in the $2 middle blind and pick up a hand whose exact contents are unimportant. I call 3 more dollars and the big blind raises to $20 straight. Two other players call and I decide to call. The flop does not help me; it is Q-8-3 of three different suits. I check, and the big blind bets $45 into an $80 pot. The other two players fold and it's up to me. I know the bettor to be an aggressive player who might take a shot at the pot with an overpair. I decide to make a bluff at the pot and raise $125 more. My opponent fidgets and asks me how much I have left; it is about $300. He agonizes and finally throws his hand away. This type of bluff is unusual for me. Normally, I would have a queen in my hand for this type of bet. Top pair is a much better bluffing hand than nothing, simply because it considerably reduces your chances of running into the nuts. Another point; the fact that I had enough money left for another "barrel" to fire (a follow-up big bet) is a critical factor in inducing a fold. Most of the time, if I got called on my raise, I would not follow up with a big bet on the fourth street. However, if I smelled a good chance of success with a big bet, then I would make it. My opponent is therefore facing the possibility that even if he calls my $125 bet, he will have to call another $300 before he finds out whether I'm bluffing. The natural human tendency in this situation is for the opponent to let go of a small pot instead of risking the loss of a big one, unless he feels very strongly you're bluffing. In pot-limit poker, it's the potential second barrel that intimidates surrender.

Hand #4—I pick up 8♥-7♥-5♠-4♣ and decide to vary my game by opening for the maximum bet. I get two callers behind me and another call from the big blind. The flop is A♥-7♦-5♣. The player in front of me leads right out for $65 into an $80 pot. This is an unusual play, as with a big hand he would be more likely to check, hoping I—the raiser—would bet the flop and middle the other two players. I have bottom two pair and a belly straight draw, which is not exactly King Kong. However, I raise the maximum, hoping the field will put me on three aces because I initially raised the pot. Everybody, including the original bettor, folds without much thought. Perhaps I actually had the best hand—my opponent could have had a straight draw—but I feel like I have run a successful bluff.

Hand #5—I pick up a hand far more powerful than my normal assortment; A♠-A♥-8♠-6♣. I open for $20 (the maximum) and get three callers, two behind me and one in front. The flop is a reasonable one to my hand, 7♠-2♥-2♦. I'm mentally prepared to bet, but the player in front of me leads for $50. With that ragged a flop, a player who flops a set normally would check and let the raiser bet. What is my opponent doing? After some thought I decide to fold, for a couple of reasons. First, there are two players behind me who might have gotten a lucky flop. They are loose players who are a lot more likely than I to be holding a deuce, and two sevens in the pocket is always possible. Secondly, the bettor is a stranger, and I don't like to get involved in a big pot with a stranger on marginal values. After all, the man may be simply betting his hand.

INSIDE MY HEAD

I would like to tell you whether my judgment was correct, but everyone folded and the bettor never revealed his holdings.

Hand #6—I pick up A♣-9♣-7♥-7♦, and call a $5 bet. The button raises, and both blinds call. I make a dubious call, and the player on my left calls, so five of us are in the pot. The flop comes K♣-Q♣-3♥, giving me the nut flush-draw. The first two players check, and it is up to me. I will bet the nut flush draw any time there is a fair chance everyone will fold, but a flop with two facecards in a multihanded raised pot looks far too dangerous to fire at, so I check. The flop is checked by all, and the dealer (Mike, one of my golfing buddies) produces the J♣, giving me an ace-high flush which is the nuts. It's checked to me; I bet $100 and get two callers. Mike turns off the J♦, pairing the board. He keeps a poker face, but knows full well that card has cost me the pot. The man in front of me checks, I of course check, and the man behind me ventures a $100 bet. The player who checked now comes over the top for a $500 raise, and we both fold. The raiser obviously had flopped a set of kings or queens. His play of checking the flop nearly cost him the pot. I am now bemoaning my hard luck, forgetting the flush I hit on the last card to win a big pot earlier in the session. The next day I "forget" to call Mike for a golf game. Of course, I am not mad at him for something that happens over which he has no control. I just don't want to be reminded of this unlucky hand while I'm watching him putt.

Hand #7—I am in the blind and pick up A♠-J♠-6♥-4♦. The flop comes down K♣-10♦-5♣, and everyone checks. The next card is the 3♦, which gives me an open-end straight draw in addition to the gutshot queen that will also make me a straight. There are twelve possible straight cards, but three of them are clubs which will make a potential flush on the board. The man on my right bets, and I call happily. The reason I am happier than my holdings would warrant is the fact that I have position on an opponent in a situation where the last card is surely going to look threatening to him. Any card except a 9—unless the board pairs—creates a possible straight.

192

Whether I actually will try to represent a straight if the last card doesn't make my hand is a bridge yet to be crossed. I'm going to fire chips in this situation—lots of them—far more often than game theory would dictate, because my opponent is a careful player who has been running badly as of late and is getting a little low on ammunition. He's also an acquaintance of mine, but I'm not going to let that stop me from stealing a pot from him. Heck, I've got to pay bills just like he does. Anyway, an offsuit 8 comes on the end, making me the nuts. He makes a small bet, I raise, and he reraises. The dealer, unmindful of the situation, starts to bring our neatly stacked chips into a jumbled mess in the center of the pot. I holler at the dealer to leave the chips alone, and place my hand on the table. Of course, it is a split pot, and the dealer would have burned up about half a minute restacking the chips if I had not said something.

Hand #8—I pick up A♠-K♦-Q♠-4♥ in late position and raise the pot. There are two callers, and the flop comes 8♠-7♦-4♠, giving me third button and the nut flush draw. My opponents check and I decide to bet. I get a caller, and the 8♦ comes on the turn, pairing the board. My opponent checks, but does so in a manner that looks to me as if he is not thrilled about the card. I don't have much of a hand, and could be drawing dead if I'm wrong, but I follow my hunch and make a big bet. My opponent caves in and folds, and I win a satisfying pot.

Each of these hands has its own little lesson, but cumulatively there is a common thread among them. I have won over $300 this session on a not particularly lucky set of deals. My style is definitely on the aggressive side. My play has not been flawless. Indeed, my excessive aggressiveness early in the session cost me about half my chips—but overall the result has been positive. There were several pots where a questionable bet won me a nice pot, and a cautious check might have been fatal, giving my opponent a free card to beat me or exposing me to a steal. All in all, I feel very much like my profit is the result of earnest labor!

TOURNAMENT PLAY

Is poker as played in tournaments pretty much the same game as when played for money? Most observers feel there are substantial differences between tournament and money-game strategy. I agree.

Certain poker players have done much better in money games than tournament play. A few people in this category are Chip Reese, Ray Zee, and David Hayden. There are a lot of fine tournament players who have much less spectacular results in money play. Some examples of tournament stars in the nineties would be Phil Helmuth, T. J. Cloutier, John Bonetti, Bobby Turner, and Tom McEvoy.

It is rare to see a player who is excellent at both forms, such as 1986 World Champion Berry Johnston, 1987-88 World Champion Johnny Chan, or 1995 World Champion Daniel Harrington. Evidently there are considerable differences between money-game play and the tournament arena.

The contrast in styles between cash-game players and tournament players is quite pronounced. As a group, the tournament players are less disciplined and more aggressive. For example, Three-time World Champion Stu Ungar plays tournament no-limit hold'em like a near maniac. He raises a lot of pots, and backs up his money by continuing to bet throughout the deal. If he runs into a big hand early, down the tubes he goes. But quite often, such a player successfully steal lots of pots and/or makes a few hands, and accumulates a freightload of chips. Then he can afford to lose a hand and not get broke. The other tournament stars I mentioned may not be outright betting maniacs, but still are much more aggressive than the top money-game players.

Why is aggression more important in tournament play than money play? Here are a couple of reasons for this:

(1) The betting structure is higher in tournament play. I am referring to the ratio in size between the antes-and-blinds and

the amount of money a player has in front of him. In tournaments you are likely to be playing $25-$50 blind with only $500-$2000 worth of chips. In a money game it is more likely you would have $2000-$5000 for blinds this high. This ratio of chips to blinds in tournaments means that there is more emphasis on preflop and on-the-flop betting, because often you are all-in before fourth and fifth street roll around. Therefore, position is less important, because you cannot use position for all the betting rounds.

Stealing ante and blind money is crucial at tournament play, because the amount your stack is increased becomes quite significant. Nobody holds great cards all day long. (At least, I never do.) You have got to stay alive during those dead spots where the cards aren't running. An occasional hijacking of the antes and blind money with virtually no hand is a necessary part of tournament play.

(2) Tournament play is psychologically different. Lose one hand, and you can be history (unless it is an event that allows rebuys). Most of the time, play is tighter at a tournament table than is the norm at money play. Most money games don't start out as barn-burners; some of the players get stuck and start steaming. In a tournament the players who are "stuck" have been forced to "report to the rail" (as the Italian Stallion would say).

Fortunately for us pros, a lot of tournament entrants are not trying to win the event. Their desire is to sneak in for umpteenth place, get back a few bucks, and talk about how a World Champion unsuccessfully tried to bluff them into laying down two kings. Some are not even trying to win prize money, but simply to last until the dinner break, or some other such low-sighted goal.

Tournament events at poker are not structured to pay off like most sporting events. At poker, first and second places are awarded a hugely disproportionate share of the prize fund. This is partly because of tradition (in the old days the number of entries was much smaller), and partly because the sponsor's publicity department feels that it is far more important psychologically for the winner's share to be a gigantic amount.

The prize fund structure dictates that you play for a high place, not just to come in the money. This means being willing to risk getting knocked out in order to get your mitts on a lot of chips. Most people try to survive at all costs. This gives the edge to those of us who are willing to play a little bolder. When I sit down in a tournament, the last thing I want is to play for a long time with few chips. Time equals money, and my time is better spent in a cash game than wasted by staying alive to finish just out of the money, or even booking a minuscule profit.

Some poker writers try to convince the survivalists that they are doing the right thing by not jeopardizing their whole stack. I believe this philosophy to be hogwash. If you look at the way top tournament players handle their chips, it sure looks like they agree with me. Jack Keller, who has had some spectacular runs of success in tournament play, is a good example. "If I have a [good] hand, I play it," says Keller, meaning he will back it with his stack in a very committal manner. You can't win a tournament unless you get all the chips. If you can show me how to garner all the chips without jeopardizing your stack, I'm curious to hear your explanation. But please bring some references, because railbird chatter is not what I'm hot to hear. I prefer to follow someone with a proven track record.

Now that we have talked in generalities, let us look at how this translates into playing specific holdings. This discussion will assume we are playing in a no-limit hold'em tournament event. The way to analyze strategy is to look at medium-good hands in various settings. You don't learn much from talking about hands at the ends of the spectrum such as 7-5 suited or a pair of kings.

When I pick up hands with two big cards such as A-K or A-Q in a money game, I vary my play. I might limp in or might raise. If the opponent indicates a strong holding by a big raise or reraise, my inclination is to dump the hand unless my stack is short. (My stack is not likely to be short in a money game, because I like to buy in for an amount 80 or 100 times the bring-in. If I lose a significant number of chips in a pot, I normally replenish my ammo when it is time to play the button.)

At tournament play I am much more aggressive with A-K and A-Q. My normal play is to raise the pot if I am the opener. If I do vary my game by limping in up front, it is with the intention of playing back if someone raises me. Please don't think that I play like an automaton, because there are certain rocks that shouldn't be given any action, and a raise by one of them is a sure sign of a through ticket. Sometimes I even have to dump A-K. The moving in of all your money with this hand is done with the hope of not getting called. When there is no hope of that, it is anti-percentage to move in if you have a reasonable amount of chips. The point I am making is when I do limp with A-K or A-Q in a tournament, it is with the intention of moving in on most people who raise me.

Hands with good suited cards other than A-K and A-Q should be played committally or folded, if the tournament is in the later stages of play where the antes or blinds are very high in proportion to the amount of money in front of you. I'm talking about A-J suited, A-10 suited, K-Q suited, K-J suited, Q-J suited, et cetera. In other words, it is rare for me to limp with these kind of hands when there is a large amount of money in the pot. I'm going to either open with a raise or fold, depending on my chip situation, hand strength, position, and who is still left to act.

What is the point to raising with a hand like K♠-J♠? In tournament play, it is important to make a play for that blind and ante money. The cost each round in overhead is quite high. Since you can't go into your pocket to keep a reasonable amount of chips in your stack, the only alternative is to raid the pot. The other competitors of course know this, and are more likely to bully a limper at tournament play than in a money game. For money, most opponents say to themselves, "Why get involved on a mediocre hand?" At tournaments they are almost **forced** to get involved on mediocre hands. That is why you must deal from strength. If you act tough, only the very tough will try to push you around. If you act weak, it's hard to keep the sand out of your eyes.

Many of these tournament decisions will be different depending on whether there is ante money in the pot to supplement the blinds. If you have seven thousand dollars in front of you and the game's structure is $50 ante, $100 and $200 blind, there is the prospect of increasing your stack by about ten percent simply by winning the ante and blind money. Go for it. If the structure is $100-200 blind without an ante, you are only increasing your stack by less than five percent. Be careful. The general rule is it's okay to chase after a lot of money with bold play, but don't chase a nubbin with all your dough.

Medium-size pairs are difficult hands to play in a tournament. In a money game, my usual strategy is to enter the pot as cheaply as possible and hope to flop a set. If someone raises me a large amount, my pair goes into the muck. In a tournament, you can't be such a fraidy-cat. People are raising with weak hands and apprehensive hearts. It is hard to help a pair, so you must make a decision as to whether you have the best hand. It is really rare for me to call someone with a medium-size pair. I move in if I think there is a reasonable chance my hand is good, and fold if it looks like my hand is beaten. Many factors go into this decision. Here are some:

(1) Who raised me?
(2) What is his frame of mind?
(3) What is his position?
(4) What is the chip situation?
(5) How will this pot affect the tournament standings.
(6) Is there a good money game going on if I get knocked out?
(7) Am I in a seat that is next to a smoker?

The point is you must make a decision as best you can when holding a pair. The worst thing to do is to have "hummingbird balls" and call hoping your opponent will either check the flop, no overcards will come, or you will turn a set. Your decision how to play a pair should come before the flop, not after the flop.

Of major consideration in the later stages of tournament play is your chip position relative to the other players, and how many places the tournament pays. My favorite stage of a tournament for garnering chips is just before the field has been narrowed to all money-winners. The way you play depends on your chip position. With a small stack you must get in there and try to win a pot. Your best chance is to pick a spot where nobody else is in yet and shove that stack into the pot hoping everybody folds. Even winning only the money in the pot at the start is a major achievement, and may carry you to a higher payoff spot. This is better than taking a mediocre hand and calling someone else's bet hoping to get lucky. Even if your hand turns out to be a little better than your opponent's, hands of this nature are easily outdrawn.

When you have a lot of chips, you can really play poker. Even though you don't want to play a big pot against one of the other leaders, don't go into a shell. I like to push the other big stacks around if they let me. They are afraid of tangling with another chip leader, because they could get busted if they gamble, but will come into the money somewhere if they don't. I like to kick a little sand in their face and see how they handle it. I will not actually play a big pot with another big stack without my holding a big hand, but I will make small probing bets, and continue to muscle anyone who refuses to ever take a stand.

As for the short stacks, I'll play a pot with one of them at the slightest excuse. Even though we each put what is actually the same amount into the pot, he has really in a sense laid me odds. He is risking everything he's got, and I am not. His chips were worth more to him than mine were to me.

You can see that I believe it is necessary to make radical changes in your approach to the game in tournament competition. Solid money-game play may let you survive and finish ninth if you hold good hands, but it won't carry you to the top. An inspection of tournament crosstables should assure you that fortune favors the bold!

A SATELLITE TIP

I have had a lot of opportunities to watch people engaging in satellite tournament play. A characteristic of satellites is the blinds becoming extremely high in relation to the amount of chips in play, especially for the finalists. I have seen an extraordinary number of mistakes made late in satellite play.

Lets talk about a common situation. Suppose in a hold'em game it is your big blind for $200, which represents half your total stack of $400. Everybody folds around to the little blind, who raises the pot. What is the minimum hand you need to call?

(a) An ace or any pair
(b) Any card jack or higher
(c) Two cards

If you answered (a), I recommend taking some Ex-lax. If you answered (b), cut the dosage in half. Only answer (c) is correct. It is a mistake to look at your hand! You should simply call the bet blind, have the dealer put five board-cards in the middle of the table, and then turn your hand up to see who wins the pot.

To see why you have an automatic call, let's look at things from the raiser's perspective. He is a quarter of the way in already. The little blind is $100 (half the big blind), and $300 more will either get him the pot or five board-cards. Even if he knows for sure he is getting called, he clearly should raise your blind hand with any hand that is average or better. This means such rags as Q-6 or J-8 are actually automatic raising hands. If there is any reasonable chance that the big blind will fold, it is worthwhile and correct to raise on a 3-2.

My practice is to raise on any two cards against a stranger, and everything except a real horror show against someone who knows enough not to look at his hand. In other words, I would raise a sure caller on 10-4 or 8-7, and fold a 9-2 or 6-3. Such situations are susceptible to exact mathematical analysis, and computer buffs are invited to write in and tell us the exact breaking point between raising and folding.

After looking at the situation from the raiser's perspective, it should be easy to see why the big blind has an automatic call. He is getting three to one on the money, because the pot contains three bets, and it is only one bet more to call. Most hold'em match-ups allow the weaker hand to be less than a 3-1 dog. For example, these match-ups all leave the better hand winning less than three-quarters of the time: A-K vs 8-6, K-Q vs K-2, 8-8 vs 10-3, et cetera. To be better than a 3-1 favorite, you need a pocket pair bigger than both your opponent's cards. As we have seen, the raiser is pretty unlikely to have that good a hand.

The situation we have been discussing reminds me of a poker story that occurred back in the seventies. A Dallas poker player known for his wild play got stuck twenty grand in a shorthanded hold'em game. It was close to quitting time, and the man decided to try and get even on one hand. He put up twenty thousand in the big blind! Everyone folded up to the little blind, who happened to be a former poker pro and World Champion—and is now a casino president. The little blind looked down and found a K-4 offsuit. This looked to be an above-average hand against a blind man, so Bobby Baldwin called the twenty grand. He won the forty thousand dollar pot with a king high, as his opponent had started with a worse hand and failed to help! I think a little transfusion of this kind of gambling blood would help many satellite players. When the blinds are super-high, you are often compelled to take a chance on revoltingly bad cards—if you look at all.

SATELLITE STRATEGY

A satellite poker tournament is a contest to win an entry into a larger tournament. Most satellite tournaments are one-table events where first place is the only finishing position that receives a prize. Our discussion will confine itself to this type of satellite, as a multi-table satellite that pays several places is more like a regular tournament in nature.

Any time you change the scoring system for a game, it is necessary to make an adjustment in the strategies you use. Satellites are sufficiently different from a regular tournament event to require a rethinking of some of the methods employed.

Those of you who compete regularly at tournament poker are aware of how important it is to knock opponents out of the event when you have reached the final table. The reason this is important is that it is possible to win a prize, sometimes a pretty good-sized prize, by simple survival, without ever accumulating a large number of chips. This applies to any event that pays more than one place. Any time someone gets knocked out of the event, it improves your own chances, even if you did not get any of the chips.

A winner-take-all tournament is different. The only way you can get a prize is to "pay" for it with the chips you have won. It is important to realize that even though the last two or three players sometimes make a deal, this does not change the nature of a winner-take-all tournament. If there are three players left, and two of the players have nearly all the money, it is unlikely that a deal will be made, and the third player wouldn't get much if a bargain was struck. Even a world champion is not going to intimidate his adversaries if he only has a couple of chips left.

To illustrate my point about the different strategy needed for a winner-take-all tournament, let me propose a hypothetical question. Suppose you are in a satellite tournament that started with ten players, each getting $300 worth of chips, so the total number of chips in play is three grand. (this is a common format for satellite play.) Through your devastatingly skillful play, you have amassed half the chips ($1500). My question is, "Would you rather have the remaining $1500 all in the hands of one player, or divided among three other players, each with $500?" Naturally, if the event paid more than one place, you would want only one other player, since this cinches second place for you. But here, second place pays zero. Is anything gained for you by having fewer players? No. I cannot see where it is any easier to beat one opponent out of fifteen hundred than three players out of five hundred apiece. So remember that your goal in a satellite event is to accumulate all the chips, not to outlast most of the other players.

Perhaps this is a timely moment to discuss the practice of a portion of the players at a one-table satellite to have a small pool of money taken up in a voluntary special collection and awarded for second place. Naturally, you must have kicked in to the collection to be eligible to win this pool money. Thus, it is quite possible that the person who actually finishes second in the satellite will not be involved in the pool, so the highest finish among the pool members will get the cheese.

The strategy for lasting the longest (yet not winning first place) is quite different than the strategy for amassing all the chips. To survive, you avoid confrontations and risk-taking as much as you can, hoping for an obviously favorable situation before doing battle. A bluff is something to be avoided if possible. I believe that getting involved in a pool that rewards survivalist tactics reduces your chances of winning the satellite. Pool members give up a little something to non-pool members because they have an incentive to employ a less-than-optimum strategy for winning the satellite. A person who wants to be a successful competitor—it doesn't have to be at poker—should not be doing anything that causes him/her to lose focus on the primary task. Michael Jordan does not make a side bet with Scotty Pippen on who is going to score the most points in the Bulls game that night. Even a bet of an inconsequential amount like five bucks would be an unacceptable distraction.

The fact is many satellite entrants play as if they had a side bet with someone on who can last the longest. They very seldom bluff, and don't risk chips unless they have either a short stack or a big hand. My friend, the event normally lasts less than two hours. It is not that easy to get the nuts. A good satellite player is a good improviser, a person who hopes to beat the hand his opponent actually holds, instead of nearly all the hands his opponent might conceivably have. Good money poker players come in a variety of styles; good satellite poker players do not. You must be aggressive to win satellites.

Yes, aggression at the key moment is a necessity. However, that moment is in he later stages of play, and not in the early stages. Let's talk about this a bit.

The typical satellite format for hold'em is to have ten entrants. These players get three hundred dollars worth of chips apiece. The blinds start out at five and ten dollars, and go up—usually doubled—every fifteen or twenty minutes. So at the start, there are nine other players competing for a pot whose chips are only five percent of your full stack. How are you supposed to play in a many-handed game with a tiny pot? Tight, tighter, and tightest. Don't get into a big fight over nothing unless you are a strong favorite to win.

There is another element of satellite play that also dictates tight play at the start. Take a look at those other nine entrants. What you rate to see at a typical table is three tough players, three average players, and three people that you have never seen before in your life. Of the three strangers, one will be so scared that you won't ever play a pot with him, and the other two will play like they are double-parked. With those two loosies, you are liable to get called if they have as much as king-high. They are not worried, because they "Didn't expect to win anyway," or "Want to see how you are playing." Besides, they can enter another satellite in a few minutes when they bust out in this one. The obvious correct strategy for the early stage of play is to do nothing fancy and simply wait for a good hand.

You will not be waiting long for the situation to change markedly. Often, half the field disappears by the time the blinds are raised for the first time, and most of the crazies figure to be gone. You are now playing in a five-handed game, and the blinds constitute ten percent of your stack instead of only five percent (unless you were lucky enough to snag a pot). It is time to play a little poker. Come out of that shell and get ready to gamble.

By this time you have had an opportunity to size up the other players. These people are also probably going to be gambling. They don't figure to be holding a rock hand any more than you do. So if you get something reasonable like top pair, don't be making a big laydown.

One fact about hold'em that is of critical importance for the late stages of satellite play is that it is hard to get a large overlay before the flop. Pair over pair and suchlike is rare. The typical layout is more like A-Q vs K-9. Sure, the A-Q is favored, but not by as big a margin as many people think; it is less than a 2-to-1 favorite. There are plenty of spots in later stages of satellite play where you get caught trying to steal the blind money and now simply have to put the rest of your dough in and hope to draw out. There are also going to be a fair number of times where you reluctantly go with your hand hoping to improve and actually have the best hand already. So don't be gun-shy before the flop. A typical situation when the table has shrunk to three finalists is for the players to each have about a grand in chips, and the blinds to now be at least $50 and $100. Any time the blinds are ten percent of your stack and you are posting two out of three deals, you don't have much flexibility. A hand like Q-9 looks more than reasonable, and an ace is a monster. So be sure to readjust your hand value scale if you get to be a finalist.

As you can see, the most important quality of the skilled satellite player is the mental flexibility to adjust to the current situation at the table. In the space of less than an hour, you go from a rock to an aggressive player to a kamikaze pilot. The reward is nice. An average satellite player rates to win one out of ten satellite tournaments; a top player rates to win about two out of ten satellite tournaments. (If you don't believe this, I hope that you are around to bet me the next time I play in a series of pot-limit Omaha satellites.)

WHAT IS YOUR PLAY?

     This is a satellite tournament poker problem presented by a moderator (me) to a blue-ribbon panel of top poker players. The panelists will give their preferred play and the reasoning behind it. The answer given is the play that person feels will work out best in the long run. Naturally, the decision might differ in actual practice if the adversary were known to you, or playing in a manner markedly different from what would be considered normal.

     This problem has been taken from actual play. You are playing in a one-table satellite tournament trying to win a seat in the 1997 World Series of Poker $2000 buy-in no-limit hold'em tournament. There are three other players remaining. The total of $8000 worth of chips in play is split pretty evenly among the four of you. The blinds are scheduled to go up every ten minutes, and have just been raised to the $200-400 level. You have $1900 in chips, and are now required to use $400 of this to post the big blind, leaving you with $1500 remaining. Your hand is a K-Q offsuit. The player on your immediate left opens with an all-in bet of $1950 ($50 more than you started with). The button and little blind fold, and it is up to you. Do you call all-in with your remaining $1500 or fold?

     Our panelists for this problem are an outstanding group of experts on no-limit hold'em. To list all their achievements would take many pages. In alphabetical order they are:

T. J. Cloutier, 2nd place finisher, 1985 World Championship, and co-author of the new book, "Championship No-limit & Pot-limit Hold'em."

Russ Hamilton, 1994 World champion.

"Action Dan" Harrington, 1995 World Champion.

Bobby Hoff, 2nd place finisher, 1979 World Championship.

WHAT IS YOUR PLAY?

Steve Lott, 4th place finisher, 1989 World Championship.

Tom McEvoy, 1983 World Champion, and co-author of the new book, "Championship No-limit & Pot-limit Hold'em."

Here are our panelist's decisions and reasoning:

Cloutier – "Fold. The most likely hands for my opponent are an ace or a pair, neither of which can I beat. "

Hamilton – "Fold. I can find a better spot for my money. I'm going uphill here."

Harrington –"Call. I like the action."

Hoff – "Call. You are getting acceptable pot odds against an ace with an undercard and good odds against an underpair. You might have him in bad shape. The only enemy hands where you're totally buried are pocket aces or kings.

Lott – Call. I would make this play without a second thought. I've seen the kind of crummy hands a lot of these satellite players move all-in with."

McEvoy – "Fold. I can't beat ace-rag, his most likely hand. The first player is the one who moved all-in, so he is more likely to have something reasonable. I would bet all-in with this hand without a problem, but it is not a good hand to call with."

DISCUSSION

I actually held that hand. My decision was to call. The result would have surprised none of our panelists. My opponent held an ace-rag offsuit. I failed to improve and lost the pot. The right "results play" was to fold.

WHAT IS YOUR PLAY?

One thing that must be emphasized on this problem is that a satellite tournament pays only first place. Were the situation the last four people in a tournament that paid multiple places, my decision would have been to abandon ship, and I expect the panelists who called here would also change their decision. In a regular tournament paying multiple places, survival is very important. You avoid confrontations, and so do the other players. So there is a penalty for finishing only fourth. The player who moves all-in on you is more likely to have a good hand in that circumstance.

There is some math that is pertinent to this problem. You are getting $2500 to $1500 pot odds, which is 5 to 3. This means you need to win 37.5 percent of the time to be making the right play mathematically. A king-queen offsuit is about 42 percent against ace-rag offsuit and about 38 percent against ace-rag suited. And against an underpair you are nearly even money. So if the opponent has the type of hand all our panelists felt was the most likely, a call is quite reasonable.

I feel a very important question is, "If your opponent does not hold ace-rag or an underpair, are you more likely to have the best of it or be buried?" There are only five hands that you would not like to face; A-A, K-K, Q-Q, A-K, and A-Q. My opinion is the same as Steve Lott's. In a satellite, there is a good chance to catch the opponent with junk. Some hands you would love to see the opponent with are K-10 offsuit or Q-9 suited, and you are about even money against hands such as 10-9 suited and suchlike. What I think Action Dan meant when he said "I like the action" is the further "against the typical satellite player's all-in hand." Frankly, compared with the kind of hands I usually hold, a K-Q looked pretty reasonable. If I did not take a stand with it, there is no telling what garbage might have been in my paw for the swan song. When the blinds are $600 every four deals and you have less than two grand in chips, patience may not be a virtue, and the other players in the contest also feel the pressure to act. My vote is cast with the callers. What is your play?

208

WORLD CHAMPIONSHIP PLAY

The World Championship Of Poker is the premiere event of our game. No other poker tournament can match the excitement generated by having four full days of play, a huge prize fund, and the title of World Champion to bestow. For all 28 years of its existence up to the time these words are being written (1997), the tournament has been held at Binion's Horseshoe in Las Vegas. I have played in this event seven times so far. My best showing was in 1987, the only year that I was fortunate enough to make it to the tremendously exciting final day of play. Immediately after the event, I wrote a series of articles on that experience. I would like to make them available here for you to read. Up to now, nobody has written anything comparable, as those who have won high prizes in this tourney have not expressed their feelings in print.

This is not so much of a "how to" type of chapter. Rather, it is to give you a good sense of the drama that is connected with the World Championship. I hope by reading it you will capture the intense feeling that goes with competing for the most coveted prize in poker, and why I consider winning third place in the 1987 World Championship Of Poker to be the most exciting thing that I have ever experienced in my life.

THE 1987 WORLD CHAMPIONSHIP
by Bob Ciaffone

1 – THE PRELUDE

Johnny Chan is the new World Champion of Poker. Most of you have seen the picture of him being awarded $625,000 for first place in the Binion's Horseshoe tournament. I would like to take you behind the scenes, and let you feel what it is like to compete for the World Championship. Each year there is a fascinating story behind the photograph of the winner and his prize money. In this year's tournament I am privileged to be able to give you a firsthand report.

The 1987 World Championship event paid thirty-six places. This had profound implications on the play. To a guy that only has a relatively small investment in a satellite tournament, the sum of seventy-five hundred dollars—the prize for 28th through 36th place—looked like a quite reasonable goal. However, I had done well in the side games, and pocketed a sizable amount of money for taking fourth place in the Pot-limit Omaha tournament, so I was not one of those players trying to earn enough to pay the rent. My sight was set on the highest goal; winning the title of World Champion. This is not to say I had any expectation of coming as close as actually occurred.

This year was my "senior year" of playing in The Big One. I won a satellite tournament at the Bingo Palace to play in 1982. In 1985 and 1986, my friends backed me with enough money to play. In my "freshman" and "sophomore" years, I had made it to the last three tables, but with poor chip position. In my "junior" year (last year), I was eliminated early on the second day. This was all before the prize format was changed to pay a lot further than just the last table. I had won many a penny for those efforts in previous outings.

2 - THE BIG ONE

Opening day of The Big One (The World Championship $10,000 Buy-in No-limit Holdem Tournament at Binion's Horseshoe in Las Vegas) has a festive air, something like a marathon race where everybody is all smiles, jokes, and laughter, but knows there is a very tough road ahead.

There are only two kinds of poker players in the world; those that play in the World Championship event, and those that wish they were playing. Belonging to the former group gives a man the feeling that he has accomplished something tangible at poker.

My initial table assignment was fairly tough, but there was no "gunner" in the group. A gunner is my term for a player who is very active with his chips, betting and raising far more than random distribution of cards would indicate a man to be holding a superior hand. Some of the world's greatest players are gunners. Players with that style include two-time World Champion Stu Ungar (the most rabid of this group), 1985 World Champion Bill Smith, 1984 World Champion Jack Keller, and 1982 World Champion Jack Straus. More restrained are 1986 World Champion Berry Johnston, Dewey Tomko, 1978 World Champion Bobby Baldwin, two-time winner Doyle Brunson, and three-time winner John Moss. Our new champion, Johnny Chan, normally has a style in between these extremes, but in this tournament he played in a more quiet manner. Note that "tight" would be a horrible misnomer to describe any of these fine players; "selectively aggressive" would be more appropriate. Tight players sometimes do well in money play. The betting structure, which uses an ante for most of the way to supplement the blind money, prevents a sitter from snoozing his way to the title. My own style this year is generally considered "restrained." This inaccurate appellation comes from my being low on dough earlier this year and needing to win the rent money, and therefore playing snugly in money games. Nobody who watched me play for four days in this year's World Championship would dream of describing my play as restrained, particularly on the final day.

My start in the tournament's first hour was inauspicious. I flopped top two pair when Utah's Dale Conway turned bottom set. Dale slowplayed the hand, failing to break me, but he knocked me down to about $7,500 in chips (from the original $10,000). After that near-disaster I held some hands and ran my chips up to around $20,000.

Late in the day I played a big pot against Dewey Tomko. I raised the pot on the button with an A-5 offsuit (don't emulate me), and Dewey called. The flop came down 8-3-2 of three different suits. Dewey knuckled his hand, and I said to myself, "Dewey called a big raise, and probably has enough of a starting hand to call me if I bet into that ragged board." I defaulted my position as the raiser and checked it back. This decision bore an unexpected but pleasant dividend. A four jumped off the deck on the turn card to make me a wheel. Dewey bet two thousand, and I said to myself, "Perhaps if I put in a big raise, he'll play me for trying to run him off the hand." A two-flush had been created by the turn card, and more by what he runs into than what he holds himself. The killers are when you have A-Q in the little blind and the big blind holds A-K, or when you turn top pair or an overpair and run into a set, and so forth. My own holdings were actually below average the first couple of days! I held aces once each day, and kings once in two days. I never flopped a flush, straight, or concealed set the first three days of play. Twice I flopped two pair, and one of those times was that hand against Conway where he held bottom set.

At the end of a second day's play, I had run my chips up to $143,200. There were only three other players in six figures, with Hugh Neville Todd of South Africa being the highest of them at $116,000. It was a tremendous day for me.

I know what you are thinking. Is this guy trying to tell me he led the World Championship after two days without holding good cards? Either he's putting me on, or his memory is like a sieve.

Let me explain how such a thing is possible. When I had a lot of chips, I started to muscle the game. I'd put in a big raise before the flop, or bet the flop with nothing, or reraise a raiser without having the normal requirements. My luck in not running into a big hand was absolutely phenomenal. Nobody ever seemed to have a hand that could take the heat. If I got called on the flop, one of the few outs that I needed would appear on fourth or fifth street. In the first two days of play, I never lost a pot that had over ten grand in it. Naturally, this lack of resistance emboldened my play. The more shenanigans I got away with, the more fancy stuff I tried, and my timing was beautiful.

On the second day's play, we narrowed the field to 27 remaining players. The event pays 36 places. This means a lot of players have given up hope of a high place, and are simply trying to come in the money. You menace them, and they fold all but the finest hands. They do not have any desire to bluff, for if they are caught, precious funds for survival are expended. It is a tremendous advantage to have a monster amount of chips on the second day of play, and I tried to make the most of the opportunity.

A common misconception is that the publicity during the four days of the World Championship is intense. The truth is that the first three days don't generate the kind of excitement in the

Harrington, Howard Lederer, and yours truly, Bob Ciaffone. The night before the finals, I got a massage and jogged a couple of miles, but still had to take a mild sleeping pill. We were all instructed to arrive at 10 AM—one hour before gametime—to be interviewed. I woke up feeling rested and ready to play poker. This was my only experience of having reached the last day's play. The media attention on "Judgment Day" more than made up for the general inattention of the first three days. We were being filmed by ESPN for a fall special, and flashbulbs were going off like skyrockets on the fourth of July.

4 - THE FINAL DAY

The final day of the 1987 World Championship Horseshoe Tournament saw a strange lineup of players. There were three professionals: myself, Frank Henderson, and Johnny Chan. Of these, only Johnny Chan could truly be called a world-class player. The other three players were experienced amateurs: Jim Spain, Daniel Harrington, and Howard Lederer. These three could not be considered amateurs in the high class of a Jay Heimowitz or a Perry Green. One would have to say Johnny Chan's fortunes looked very bright, since he was the chip leader against players who were unaccustomed to doing battle at the exalted level of the World Championship, despite a certain amount of experience at lesser tournaments. In addition, Jim Spain, the player who was nearest to challenging Chan for the lead, was on Johnny's immediate right.

I have reported to you that my card-holding the first three days were nothing special—although the holdings of my opponents was decidedly subpar. On the last day, my card-holding was very good. Oh, I only held an average amount of really big hands. I had aces once, kings once, queens once, and ace-king suited once. On the other hand, my number of playable starting hands was quite high. A man needs some excuse to get in there and fight for the pot. I held a lot of hands such as A-10, A-rag suited, and two nines. Since I was playing moderate hands in a very aggressive manner, I had at least a decent base to work from in getting involved.

WORLD CHAMPIONSHIP PLAY

Many people, including me, thought that Chan would play very aggressively at the last table, in view of his natural style, relatively weak opposition, and position as chip leader. For some reason, Johnny started out playing in a very restrained manner. I have not talked to him about this, so I do not know why this happened. Perhaps he held poor cards, or perhaps he didn't want to build big pots and give Lady Luck a chance to derail the Orient Express (his media-bestowed nickname).

Nobody else at the table seemed inclined to force the pace of play, so I simply filled a void that was created. I did a lot of betting and raising, and like in previous days, I wasn't meeting much resistance. My chips grew steadily throughout the afternoon. I went from $147,000 to $300,000, then $400,000, and then to half a million. Johnny Chan did not watch this happen with complete equanimity. At one point, he said disgustedly, "Don't you guys ever play back at him?" If Chan ever had any intention of trying to run over the game—and I don't think he did—the opportunity disappeared when the chips at the table went from people underneath him to the man who had position on him.

Despite the fact that I was rolling along like a freight train, I tried to stay as far away from tangling with Johnny Chan as I could. We never played a big pot until the game got down to threehanded. By this time I had in the neighborhood of half the chips in play.

When the game shrank to threehanded, it was no longer possible for me to run over it. Frank Henderson and Johnny Chan were determined to stop me, and it looked like the opposition was finally going to make a stand.

At this point the first hand in the history of tournament poker to contain more than a million dollars in it came up between myself and Chan. There has been a lot of talk about this hand, some of it critical of me. Here is what happened, as I remember it. I picked up the A♥–4♥ in the little blind. We were playing threehanded with a $2,000 ante and blinds of $10,000 and $20,000. Johnny Chan called twenty thousand on the button, and I raised the pot $85,000 more. Henderson folded, and Chan called me quickly.

(Remember, there was $66,000 in the pot before I raised it.) This meant there was the large sum of $236,000 in the pot before the flop. The flop was K-J-4, with two spades and a club. I chose to bet $200,000 at the pot, and Chan quickly went all-in for $240,000 raise. What should I do?

The chip-position at the start of this hand was roughly Ciaffone--$687,000, Chan--$547,000, and Henderson--$276,000. If I called and lost, I would be down to $140,000. If I folded, I would still have $380,000. However, if I got lucky and won, I would have $1,244,000; Chan would be out of the tournament, and I would be a lock for the quarter-million second prize and a tremendous favorite for the crown itself. I was pretty sure Chan had a made hand and not a drawing hand, but there is always the element of doubt. It was extremely likely that an ace or a four would win the pot for me, which is five outs twice. At the table I calculated that I was about a 3 to 1 underdog and getting 3 to 1 pot odds. (This calculation was done with some people in the partisan gallery screaming things like, "Get him, Bob," which I did not let influence me.) Subsequent calculation at home shows me to be getting 3.65 to 1 pot odds, and being about a 3.75 to 1 underdog to hands such as K-9, so my heat-of-battle calculations were close to the mark. At any rate, I took the course of action that had it worked would have let me escape ever having to play Johnny Chan heads-up. I called, failed to draw out against his king-queen, and the "Orient Express" became a heavy favorite to roll on to victory.

My story is not quite over, since I won several pots in a row and ran my chips up to about a quarter of a million. I then played a pot with about a half a million in it against Chan. He had top pair, and I had second pair on the flop. A lucky card came on fourth giving me two pair, and it looked like I might be back in the thick of things, but Chan redrew to make two bigger pair on the last card, and Bob Ciaffone bit the dust. Some time later Henderson, having used up the ninth of his lives sometime previously, also got beaten by a big pot, and Johnny Chan became the 1987 World Champion. He was a bit lucky at the very end, but the truth of the matter is the best player won.

WORLD CHAMPIONSHIP PLAY

Of the amateurs at the last table, Dan Harrington's play made a particular impression on me. He had K-K against A-J and lost a huge pot to Jack Keller, and A-Q against A-6 and lost a huge pot to Jim Spain. With normal luck he would have finished much higher than 6th.

Howard Lederer plays solidly, but still needs more seasoning. However, he's only 23 years old, and obviously has great potential.

Both of these men, along with myself, are quite good at other games such as chess and backgammon. Many top games players such as Paul Magriel and Tobias Stone have taken up poker, and it only seems a matter of time before they make their mark at that game.

As for me, one must wonder whether my successes at the World Series were "the blind squirrel finally finding an acorn" or the emergence of a new poker tournament star. There is no way I or anybody else can answer that question. I will tell you this: I played better this year than I ever had in the past. Part of this is due to certain techniques I have picked up by watching some top players, particularly T. J. Cloutier, Bill Smith, and Jack Straus. Whether I will ever again be in such a good position to win the title of World Champion is problematical, but I do have some reason to expect other tournament successes in the future.

There is great joy of getting to the last table and being able to contend for the World Championship on national television. This is what makes the life of a poker player worthwhile. The stress is nothing compared to the tremendous excitement. I hope some day to have that pleasure again. Maybe you should give yourself a chance to get there and have the experience of a lifetime. For a poker aficionado, there is no better use on this planet for ten grand than an entry to the World Series of Poker, as far as I'm concerned.

This concludes my series of articles on reaching the final table of the 1987 World Championship. In the decade following this experience, I never came so close to the ultimate prize again. However, the history book is not yet closed.

218

INDEX OF POKER PERSONALITIES

INDEX OF POKER PERSONALITIES